CRIMᴇ IN HERTFORDSHIRE

Volume Two

Murder and Misdemeanours

Simon Walker

The Book Castle

First published March 2003
by
The Book Castle
12 Church Street
Dunstable
Bedfordshire
LU5 4RU

ISBN 1 903747 28 7

Printed by Antony Rowe Ltd., Bumper's Farm, Chippenham, Wiltshire, SN14 6LH

Contents

Acknowledgements

Many of those organisations and individuals who helped with the first volume of this series, *Crime in Hertfordshire: Law and Disorder,* deserve equal acknowledgement for their aid in the preparation and research for this book. Once again particular thanks are due to the following: the staff at Hertfordshire Archives and Local Studies; Rosemary Bennett, now retired, from Hertford Museum; Anne Wheeler at the Museum of St. Albans; Gill Riding and her staff at Hitchin Museum; and Alison Taylor of Wardown Park Museum in Luton, who taught me that lace making and its history is a fascinating subject in its own right. Inspector Steve Kourik of Hertfordshire Constabulary Historical Society spent a morning with me, showing me through the Society's collection. Pauline Humphries was kind enough to proof read the final draft. And finally my brother, Richard Walker, who kept his eyes open on my behalf during his eclectic browsing, and came up with some useful sources and information. Acknowledgements are due to the Ordnance Survey for permission to reproduce maps. To all those mentioned, and to others I may have missed, I should like to say thank you. Any errors are of course all my own.

About the Author

Simon Walker has lived in Hertfordshire all his life. He was born in Hitchin in 1950, and was educated at the local Grammar School. After a career in computing, security and finally customer services in the financial sector, he retired in 1999 in order to concentrate on local history. He has written three other books: *The Bridewells of Hitchin, Underground Hitchin, Hitchin: a Photographic History of Your Town*, and *Crime in Hertfordshire: Law and Disorder.*

Murder and Misdemeanour in Hertfordshire

Introduction

This collection is complementary to my earlier book, *Crime in Hertfordshire: Law and Disorder.* That volume dealt with the development of law and order from the Anglo-Saxon period to the mid twentieth century; how the law and the courts developed and functioned; the punishments inflicted on offenders; and how the forces of law enforcement grew from hue and cry to the police forces we are familiar with today.

This book is a compilation of cases either from Hertfordshire or with a very close Hertfordshire connection. One or two are quite well known, most are less so. The last chapter contains miscellaneous cases about which there is not sufficient information available to form a chapter in their own right, but which are sufficiently interesting to be worthy of inclusion.

Of necessity the bulk of the cases date from the 17th century onward, as the records of early crimes are imperfect. For many years magistrates tried minor offences, and few, if any, records were kept. In some cases Manor Courts tried trivial offenders, but for the most part they interested themselves in matters of land transfer and the like. More serious offenders appeared at the Quarter Sessions or Assize Courts, but even here the record keeping was meagre: presentments and indictments exist, sometimes with the verdict and sentence recorded, sometimes not. Some records are missing altogether. Gaol records tell us who was in gaol, and for what offence, but unless corresponding court records exist, they tell us nothing of the story behind the crime.

Later, pamphleteers and publishers of broadsheets did a roaring trade in cheap accounts of the more sensational cases, often in graphic and gory detail. Sometimes they were accurate, sometimes not. Nonetheless they are an invaluable source of information, not just about a particular crime, but also the attitudes of the time. In some respects people have little changed – the love of sensationalism is an obvious example. In other ways they seem very different. Belief in the supernatural, attitudes towards poverty and the cruelty visited upon offenders spring to mind.

With the development of newspapers we frequently find the same case reported in different publications, allowing comparisons to be made. Like the broadsheets and pamphlets, the reports were often in great detail, but now much more reliable. Later court records too are far more complete than their predecessors.

In the past, as now, most crimes were of a petty nature. Various forms of theft predominated, accounting for between two thirds and three quarters of appearances before the courts. The major differences were the type of goods stolen and the sentences handed down by the courts. To be representative, ideally a large selection of petty thefts of minor items should be included.

Whilst these minor offences are interesting in themselves, not least in the light they throw upon social history, the sensational crime beckons, and most of the offences in this book fall into that category. I have nonetheless found space for some of these petty cases in the final chapter.

If pamphlets and newspapers are to be believed, many a prisoner executed did three things; he confessed to his crime; he wrote or made an address to the public at large exhorting them to learn by his example; and thirdly, and less surprisingly, he turned to religion. In many of these confessions and addresses the prisoner suddenly acquired a remarkable erudition, which leads one to suspect that the confessions and addresses are fabricated, or at least influenced, by the authorities – frequently the chaplain of the gaol where the convicted person awaited execution.

There has to be some concern about the guilt of offenders in the early days, when forensic science was either non-existent or in its infancy. How many innocent people were convicted on evidence that would today be considered highly suspect? It is only quite recently that courts have recognised that most people's power of observation is poor. In the past, if a witness was prepared to swear in court that he recognised the man in the dock, that was usually good enough for the jury. And if a police officer said that the defendant had confessed, why then, it must be true.

On the other side of the coin, many crimes must have gone unrecognised as such, and guilty people escaped justice. It is interesting to speculate how modern techniques would have aided the constables, watchmen and the early police forces. Imagine how useful genetic analysis of samples would have been, for example, in the case of the gang rape of Sarah Dye.

The truth will never be known, but the suspicion must be that many innocent people were convicted, whilst many guilty people went free. The safety of modern convictions is not perfect, but it is better than ever it was in the past.

I have kept place-names and spellings as they appear in the sources consulted. In most cases they are the same, or at least similar, but occasionally villages have been swallowed up and roads demolished or re-named.

Of particular interest is the role of the public house in cases of violent or sudden death. In several of the cases in this book the body was taken, not to a mortuary or doctor's surgery, but to the local public house. Many of the initial inquest hearings were held there too. This may seem strange, but then many magistrates' courts, and even ecclesiastical courts, were also held in pubs. Before the formation of the county police, they even served on occasion as temporary lock ups for prisoners. Why was this? The answer is simple: if not the pub, then what other building could be used? In many smaller communities the only alternatives were private houses and farms. Thus the pub becomes the logical choice. Added to that fact, what more convivial location for what was often a sombre business? The practice fell into disuse following the Licensing Act of 1902, which stipulated that inquests were not to be held in licensed premises unless there was nowhere else to hold them.

All the maps in this book are reproduced from the Ordnance Surveys of the period 1833-1835. They were updated at different times through the nineteenth century, with the addition of such features as railways. Whilst they are not always contemporary with the events described, for consistency I chose to use the same surveys throughout. The eighteenth and nineteenth centuries saw growth in population and urbanisation, but in a rural county like Hertfordshire these were not as significant as they were in the industrial midlands or London, nor the explosive expansion of the twentieth century. Most of the features, whether of landscape or town, survived and appear on the maps.

Murder and Misdemeanour in Hertfordshire

Chapter One

Child Murder in Hatfield, 1602

Our first case is an excellent example of how important pamphlets can be in adding detail to early crimes.

From the Assize records we know that Agnes Dell and George, her son, were tried for murder, found guilty and sentenced to hang at Hertford in 1606. We know that Anthony James was their victim, that George actually did the deed with a knife (value 1d.), and that the body was thrown into a pond; we know the names of the judge and the jurors. The official record tells us little more.

Fortunately much can be discovered from two contemporary pamphlets that reveal a dreadful story:

> "The Most Cruel and Bloody Murther committed by an Innkeeper's Wife, called Annis [Agnes] Dell, and her Sonne George Dell, Foure yeeres since. On the bodie of a Childe, called Anthonie James in Bishop's Hatfield in the Contie of Hartford, and now most miraculously revealed by the Sister of the said Anthony."

> "The Horrible Murther of a young Boy three yeres of age, whose sister had her tongue cut out, and how it pleased God to reveale the offenders by giving speech to the tongules Childe. Which Offenders were executed at Hartford the 4 of August, 1606."

The James family were well-to-do, and it may have been this that attracted the robbers who broke into their home. Both parents were murdered, and their bodies were buried in the woods. The killers split up, and one group, which included a woman, took the two children, Anthony and Elizabeth, with them to the inn that the Dells ran in Hatfield. They offered Mrs. Dell part of the booty if she would take in the orphans. She agreed, and the children came to live with the Dells, albeit for a short period only.

The children cannot have known what was going on, or the Dells would not have allowed them the freedom that they did. What tale they were told to explain the absence of their parents is not recorded; whatever it was, they must have been satisfied with it, because they did not raise the alarm. Nonetheless, it was the liberty the youngsters were granted that was a major factor in the Dells being brought to justice.

A tailor, Henry Whipley, noticed two children whose clothing aroused his professional interest, especially the green jacket worn by Anthony. The children told him that they were lodging with the Dells, but when Whipley later went to the inn and asked to examine the clothing further, he was told that the children had gone.

Gone they had. During the evening following Whipley's enquiry, George Dell and some of the robbers took the children off. Anthony was gagged with cow dung, and his throat cut. His body was dumped in a pond about half a mile from the town. Elizabeth's tongue was cut out, and she was given into the care of a beggar, who agreed to take her for "a peece of money." Why the killers did not kill her as they had her brother is a mystery. The reason cannot have been mercy or squeamishness. In the event the beggar abandoned her in a hollow tree, where she was later found; but even then her ordeal was not over. True, her rescuer helped her out of the tree, but so alarmed was he by the noises she made that he abandoned her. She was unable to speak, and no-one connected her with any crime other than the removal of her tongue, nor with Hatfield. Had they done so, the appalling deeds might have been discovered earlier than they were.

Some three weeks later Anthony's body was found, and in order to identify him his coat was hung up in various local towns in the hope that someone would recognise it. Someone did: Henry Whipley went to the authorities, and told them about the two children, and how they had lodged for a short time with the Dells. Mother and son were questioned, but other than admitting that the children had stayed with them, they denied any knowledge of their fate. Though suspicions were aroused, there was not enough evidence against the innkeepers to secure a conviction. They were however bound over at succeeding Assizes.

Not long after Anthony's body was found, those of his parents were discovered. Elizabeth was still missing. The poor girl seems to have existed by begging from town to town for the next four years, until by chance she returned to Hatfield. She recognised the Dells' inn, and mimed to the gathering crowd the awful cruelties that she and her brother had suffered at the hands of the owners. Among the onlookers was Henry Whipley. Even after the lapse of four years, he recognised the girl, and it was upon his evidence the Dells were once more arrested.

Elizabeth was fostered with a local family and, with the resilience of youth, after a while she began to recover from her ordeal. She was sent to the local school, where, after imitating animal noises, she eventually recovered the power of speech; she was thus able to give evidence against the Dells.

One of the pamphlets implies that the Dells were involved in the murder of the parents, whilst the other says that they were killed by the group of vagrants. There is no way to tell which is true for certain; in the 1600's, and for several centuries afterwards, vagrants were believed to be a loose knit criminal fraternity, carrying out thefts and murders, then disbanding, only to re-form at a later date in another place to continue their predations. That poverty and vagrancy led to theft there is little doubt, but the idea of a "brotherhood" of robber-vagrants is far fetched.

If the Dells killed Mr. and Mrs. James, why did they not kill Anthony and Elizabeth straight away? We know that they were capable of killing and maiming the children. Perhaps there was a vestige of mercy in them after all; if so, what prompted the appalling brutality that they later showed to the youngsters? Could it have been Henry Whipley's innocent enquiries that precipitated the crime?

Wherever the truth lies, it was for the murder of Anthony that the Dells were publicly hanged on 4 August 1606.

Chapter Two

Jane Norcott & the Bleeding Finger, 1629

The bizarre sequence of events surrounding the death of Jane Norcott in 1629 has never been fully explained, and probably never will be. Perhaps the best thing to do is present the information as it appeared in print, under the title of "Account of a Murther in Hertfordshire, in the 4th Year of King Charles I, Taken in Writing from the Depositions, by Sir John Maynard, Serjeant at Law." Sir Nicholas Hyde tried the case.

Bear in mind that at that time the supernatural was a part of everyday life. For centuries past, and for many years still to come, the majority of the population firmly believed that they were surrounded by demons and other malignant spirits; witches sold their souls to the devil in return for the power to blight their neighbours' lives and livelihoods; and magic was reality, not a stage trick to amuse or amaze an audience.

> "Jane Norcott, the Wife of Arthur Norcott, being found murder'd in her Bed, the Coroner's Inquest on view of the body and Depositions of Mary Norcott, her Husband's Mother, Agnes his Sister, and her Husband, John Okeman, gave evidence that she was *Felo de se* [a suicide]; the said Persons giving Information, that she went to bed with her young Child, her Husband being abroad, and that nobody had been, or could come to her without their knowledge, they lying in the outer Room. But divers Circumstances manifesting that she could not murder herself, 30 Days after, the Jury pray'd the Coroner to have the Body taken out of the Grave. Whereupon they Chang'd their Verdict; and the above Persons being try'd with the Husband at Hertford Assizes, were acquitted, but so much against the Evidence, that Judge Harvey advis'd an Appeal, which was accordingly brought by the young Child against his Father, Grandmother, and Aunt, and her Husband Okeman.
> On Trial, the Minister of the Parish where the Fact was committed, depos'd, That the Body being taken up out of the Grave 30 Days after the Party's Death, and lying on the Grass, and the Four Defendants, being required, each of them touch'd the dead Body, whereupon the

10

Brow of the Dead, which before was of a livid and Carrion Colour, begun to have a Dew, or gentle sweat arise on it, which encreased by degrees, till the sweat ran down in drops on the Face: the Brow turn'd to a lively and fresh Colour; and the deceased opened one of her Eyes, and shut it again three several times; she likewise thrust out the ring or Marriage Finger three times and pulled it in again, and the Finger dropt Blood on the Grass.

Chief Justice Hyde seeming to doubt the Evidence, asked who saw it besides? To which he reply'd, That he believed the whole Company saw it, but was sure his Brother, Minister of the next parish, saw it as he did. That Person being sworn, gave Evidence exactly as above.

Other circumstantial Proof was 1. That she lay in a compos'd manner in Bed, and the Bed-clothes not disturb'd. 2. Her Throat was cut from Ear to Ear, and her Neck broke, both which she could not do herself. 3. There was no Blood in the Bed. 4. There were two streams of Blood on the Floor, but no Communication betwixt them, and turning up the Mat, there were clots of congeal'd Blood on the Straw. 5. The bloody Knife was found sticking in the Floor, the point towards the Bed. 6. There was the print of the Thumb and Four Fingers of a Left Hand. And lastly, the Prisoners before had said, no Stranger could come into the Room.

Okeman was acquitted, but the other three found guilty; the Grandmother and Husband were executed; but the Aunt was not, on account of her being with Child. Sir John adds, that they confessed nothing at the Execution."

This version differs slightly from that published in *Hertfordshire Folklore* by W. B Gerish, but most of the differences are not significant. It is worth mentioning however that in the Gerish version, Justice Hyde asked a witness how he could tell whether the handprint was from a left or right hand. Perhaps this says something about the intelligence of the judge.

The belief that a corpse could indicate the guilt of a murderer by bleeding was both old and widespread. There have been other instances where a bleeding corpse was said to have indicated guilt. During the trial of the Pendle Forest witches of Lancashire in 1612, the body of Thomas Lister was said to have bled at the touch of Jennet Preston. Just before he died, Lister had accused her of bewitching him, and she was indicted for his murder. She was tried at York, and, despite her denials, found guilty of murder by witchcraft and hanged.

The belief was held at the highest level: James VI of Scotland, later James I of England, wrote in his *Daemonologie* of 1597 that 'in a secret murther, if the dead carkasse be at any time thereafter handled by the murtherer, it will gush out of blood, as if the blood were crying to Heaven for revenge of the murtherer.'

Nor was this method of trial unique to these islands. According to some versions of the tale, the murderer of Siegfried was discovered by making the suspects walk past his body; when the assassin's turn came, the corpse dripped blood. The method of trial was common in Germany in the 15th century, where Heinrich Kramer and James Sprenger recorded it in their *Malleus Maleficarum (the Hammer of Witches),* an appalling work that contributed to the witch-hunts throughout most of Europe for more than two centuries. The two Dominican inquisitors tell us that this supernatural form of trial had been used at least since the 13th century, when it was noted by Vincent of Beauvais in his *Speculum Naturale (Mirror of Nature).*

Right: the thirteenth century Malleus Maleficarum – "The Hammer of Witches" – describes how corpses bleed in the presence of their murderers. This edition was printed in 1669.

Few people today would claim that either Thomas Lister or Jane Norcott's corpses really indicated who had killed them, so I think we must rule out divine intervention. Unfortunately the information is rather scanty, and there are a lot of questions unanswered.

There have been cases of people being pronounced dead, and buried prematurely. But if Jane Norcott was buried alive, she cannot have survived for thirty days; in any case, her injuries preclude the possibility that she was alive when she was buried. The evidence of the two parsons must therefore be inaccurate. Either they were deluded, or they were deliberately lying. But if they lied, why?

That the body cannot have indicated that three people were involved does not of course prove their innocence. Some or all of them may indeed have conspired together to kill Jane Norcott.

As far as the injuries are concerned, in spite of the belief expressed by the witnesses to the contrary, Jane could have cut her own throat. At that time it was one of the most popular means of suicide, and some of the self-inflicted injuries were both extensive and frightful. It is, however, more difficult to see how she can have broken her own neck.

Where did Jane die? The bloodstains on the floor and under the mat might indicate that Jane died there, and was put into the bed afterwards. According to the report there was no blood on the bed, but that does not prove she was not killed there - if her neck had been broken first, her throat could have been cut later. The loss of blood would not have been great. But then, how did the blood come to be on the floor and beneath the mat? Either way, it seems improbable that she killed herself. Someone else must have been involved.

It would be useful to know how secure the house was. The witnesses said that an outsider could not have entered Jane's room without being seen by the family, but is that true?

The motive is another question. What were relationships like within the household? Did they get on well, or was Jane viewed with hostility for some reason? There is no evidence that Jane was killed for financial gain, so perhaps it was a personal matter, or an act of violence in the heat of the moment.

There is much we don't know, so we can only make an educated guess at the truth; and the probability is that Jane was murdered by one or more of those who were tried, or at least with their knowledge.

A final question lies over the location of the events. The member of the clergy who gave evidence said that they had been seen by his brother from the next parish. Assuming he meant his natural brother, and not just a brother clergyman, a search of parish records for the period reveals two possibilities where the incumbents of adjoining parishes bear the same surname: Watton-at-Stone and Stapleford, and Elstree and Aldenham.

Chapter Three

The Wicked Deed of Job Wells
Hemel Hempstead, 1753

It is hard to feel much sympathy for Job Wells, though he was perhaps no more than the product of his upbringing and the society in which he lived. That he was guilty of the rape of his own daughter Maria is without doubt. That the poor girl had to testify against her own father on a capital charge compounded the tragedy.

Wells was born in about 1710, the son of poor parents, in Hemel Hempstead. He received little or no education as a boy, and about as much moral guidance. Thus by the time he married at the age of nineteen he had few prospects other than a life of rural drudgery as a husbandman and labourer.

Wells worked for many masters in and around Redbourn over the years, and had a reputation as a good and hard worker, though his behaviour in other respects left much to be desired. He was known as a heavy drinker and a womaniser, and when in his cups he revealed the worst sides of his character: he was described as being "a down-right Brute" when under the influence.

Wells' wife was a poor but hardworking woman, who as was common at the time bore him many children.

In 1752 Mrs. Wells gave birth for the last time; she died three days later. The local people blamed Wells for her death, saying that he had forced himself upon her the day after the birth. He neither confirmed nor denied the story, a stance which many saw as a tacit admission of guilt.

At the time of his trial, eight children of the family were still living; how many had died is not recorded. Infant mortality was high, especially amongst the poor working-class of which the Wells family was a part. Whether there were any children older than Maria is unknown, but if there were, they were probably boys, or had left home, because following her mother's death the girl seems to have taken on most of the household duties. In 1753 Maria was sixteen or seventeen. All we know of her appearance is that she was short for her age.

Wells' trial took place over two days, the 13th and 14 August 1753, before Sir William Lee and Sir Thomas Denison.

Maria was first sworn in as a witness, and then described what happened. Her testimony was recorded almost word for word, which was unusual at that time.

Question: Look upon the Prisoner, Do you know him?

Maria: Yes, he is my own Father.

Prisoner: Maria, take care what you say, for you have a Soul to be saved as well as I. For my Part, I am not afraid of Death.

[*At this the Witness burst into a Flood of Tears.*

Q: Child, compose yourself, and tell the Court and Jury what you have to say against the Prisoner.

Maria: One Day my Father came home very soon in the Afternoon, and went to Bed.

Q: What Day was it, and what Time?

Maria: It was the 27 of April last, about Five or Six o'Clock, my Father went to Bed, and bid me come to Bed to him; I refused; then he pulled out a Knife, and swore if I did not, he would rip me up, or cut my Throat. Then, after I had undress'd my Brothers and Sisters, I went to Bed to him.

Q: Should you have gone to Bed to him if he had not threatened you?

Maria: I should not.

Q: What happened to you after you was in Bed; you must speak out.

Maria: My Father pulled open my Legs, and got between them; then I cried out, and he threatened to kill me if I did not lie quiet; then he did so and so to me.

Q: The Law requires in this Case that you should speak out plain; you must therefore say what he did to you in plain express Words.

Maria: After he got between my Legs, he put his **** [this word is censored in the pamphlet] into me by Force, and hurt me very much.

Q: What happened after this; you must spea k out.

Maria: I felt something warm come from him into me.

Q: Did you stay in Bed with him after this?

Maria: No, I got out of Bed, and, almost naked, I got out of Doors, and went upon the Common, and there staid till I thought he was asleep, then I went home, and went to Bed to the Children.

Q: Did you complain of this to any one the next Day.

Maria: No, for my Father said if I told any Body what he had done he would kill me.

Q: Was there any thing else happened to you?

Maria: Yes, the next Night, about Nine at Night, my Father swore if I did not come to Bed with him he would kill me; and, for fear of being killed, I did go to Bed to him again, and he did the same as he did the Night before.

[Here she was obliged to repeat as before.

Q: Did you mention this to any Body the next Day.

Maria: The next Day Mary Hitchcock asked what was the Matter, that I cried out; and I told her, my Father wanted to make a Whore of me; and she said, I hope he has not; but I said, he has, indeed.

The next-door neighbour, Mary Hitchcock, testified that she had heard Maria cry out, and the next morning she approached the girl and asked if everything was all right. According to Mrs. Hitchcock's evidence, Maria told her that "her Father wanted to make a Whore of her." Mary went on:

"Said I, I hope he has not done it; he has, said she, and fell a crying, for he threatened to kill me if I did not let him. I then went to the Overseers to tell them of it, for I thought it ought to be looked into; and the Overseers sent to Dr. Law to examine her."

Next in the witness box was the Doctor, Joseph Law. His testimony was as follows:

"I am a Surgeon, and live in Redburn; on the 29 of April last I was sent for by the Overseers of the Poor, to examine Maria Wells; I did so, and found that Violence had been used to her, for her private Parts were much swelled; and that there had been a Penetration; I examined the Girl concerning it, and she said, her Father had lain with her by Force, and she farther owned to me, that she felt something come from her Father warm into her. The Overseers then got a Warrant, and had him taken up and carried before Justice Carpenter, who committed him to Hertford Gaol, and the Girl was sent to St. Alban's Workhouse."

In his defence the prisoner contradicted himself, claiming at first that he knew nothing of the charge; then that he had been drunk, and that Maria had been a willing participant. He called his sister, Patience Ivory, as a witness on his behalf. She said that she had seen Maria on the day in question, and that "she did not complain to me, and seemed to walk as well as at any other Time."

Throughout his trial, and for some time afterwards, Wells did not seem to appreciate the seriousness of the charge against him. He was reprimanded several times during the trial for his "daring and undaunted" attitude. Even when the jury returned a verdict of guilty, and Justices Lee and Denison pronounced a sentence of death, the reality of his situation did not seem to hit him.

Whether he believed that incestuous rape was normal practice we don't know. Perhaps, for him and others in the rural society in which he lived, it was. Certainly he thought that his crime was a trivial matter, and it was some time before the prison chaplain and other preachers were able to convince him otherwise. After all, he said, he had used no violence towards Maria. His fellow inmates in Hertford Gaol read to him from the Bible - he was illiterate himself – and he seemed much affected by this.

On Sunday, 26 August, Wells twice attended church. He received the Holy Sacrament, and heard a sermon on the subject of the wickedness of parents who fail in their duty to their children. The Reverend Mr. Tutty told him that by his example he had taught his children "the Practice of every kind of Wickedness." Not only that, but he had by force violated the chastity of his daughter, who it was his obligation to defend even at the cost of his life.

Following the service, Wells had the following message sent to his brother:

> "He hopes his Daughter will freely forgive him, as he freely forgives
> her, and acknowledges his Guilt; and hopes that his Children will all
> take Warning by him; and begs that his Relations and Neighbours will
> give them all the best Advice that is in their Power; he also begs of
> Mrs. Keys, at the Cock at Redburn, where his Son is, that she will give
> him the best Advice that is in her Power; and prays to God to bless all
> his Children, and hopes God Almighty will receive his Soul into his
> everlasting Kingdom."

At ten o'clock the following morning Wells was taken from Hertford Gaol to church, where before a large congregation the Reverend Mr. Bouchier preached a sermon based on Galatians, chapter 6 verses 7-8: "Be not deceived; God is not mocked; for whatsoever a man soweth, that shall he also reap. For he that soweth to his Flesh, shall of the flesh reap Corruption: but he that soweth to the Spirit, shall of the Spirit reap Life everlasting." Hardly a comforting theme for Job Wells. Mr Bouchier also took the opportunity to use the prisoner's unhappy situation to deter the audience from "giving a loose to their unruly appetites."

From the church Wells was put into a cart, where he sat on his coffin all the way to the place of execution. At the scaffold he spent some time in prayer, then addressed the crowd. He exhorted them to take warning by his crime, to which he confessed, and asked them to pray for him.

At 12:45 p.m. Job Wells was hanged for the rape of his daughter. His last words were reported to have been, "Lord, have mercy upon me."

Wells was unfortunate to have been executed for his crime, even in the eighteenth century. The death penalty for rape was by no means certain, and one cannot help thinking that the sentence was in part due to its incestuous nature.

THE

T R I A L

OF

J O B   W E L L S,

OF

Redburn in the County of *Hertford*,

FOR

A R A P E committed on the Body of his own Daughter, MARIA WELLS,

AT THE

A S S I Z E S held at *HERTFORD*,

BEFORE

The Right Hon. Sir WILLIAM LEE, Knt.
Chief Juftice of his Majefty's Court of *King's Bench*,

AND

The Hon. Sir THOMAS DENISON, Knt.
One other of His Majefty's Juftices of the faid Court,

On *Monday* the 13th and *Tuefday* the 14th of *Augaft*, 1753.

To which is added,

A full ACCOUNT of his Behaviour under Sentence, and at the Place of Execution.

And the Subftance of a moft Excellent S E R M O N, on this Occcafion, Preached before him at *Hertford*, on *Sunday* the 26th of *Augaft*.

―――――――――――――――――――――

L O N D O N:
Printed for C. CORBET, at *Addifon's Head, Fleet-Street,* 1753.
[Price Six Pence.]

Above: the front page of the pamphlet published in 1753, describing the crime of Job Wells.

What happened to Maria and the other children? We know only that they had aunts and uncles who might have taken them in. What effect the case had on Maria's future we can only speculate. There was no protection of anonymity; the case was heard in a court open to the general public; and for those who could not view the trial in person, it was reported in detail in the pamphlet available for the cost of a few pennies. Her "shame" would have been known throughout the county, and the gossips would have had a field day. From the moment that Job Wells in his drunken state surrendered to his lust, the poor girl's life would never be the same again.

Chapter Four

The Datchworth Tragedy, 1769

The poor, it is often said, are always with us. Whilst not officially criminals, for centuries they were treated in much the same manner.

A short introduction to the poor laws up to the time of the events to be described might be helpful in understanding what happened at Datchworth Green in 1769.

Before the 16th century care for the poor relied upon charity, given voluntarily by the church or the more wealthy members of the population. In 1552 parishes were required to organise the collection of alms; eleven years later contributions were made compulsory, on pain of imprisonment. After another twenty years, the parish poor rate was established as the normal means of relieving the poor, administered by overseers appointed by the Vestry.

More legislation followed:

1598   An Act for the Relief of the Poor - the main basis of English poor law until 1834. This act provided for the appointment of overseers and the compulsory levying of a poor rate in each parish for the relief of those unable to work, either because of age or infirmity. The rate was also used to purchase raw materials to provide work for the able-bodied poor. The settlement parish of a pauper was defined as their parish of birth, but could be changed by a one year period of residence elsewhere. A pauper could be returned to his or her parish of settlement.

1601   A re-enactment of the 1598 statute, with minor amendments.

1662   The Settlement Act - the period of residence required to change the settlement parish was reduced to 40 days. Parish overseers were authorised to remove newcomers to their parish of settlement if they were likely to become a financial burden to the parish.

1622   An act encouraging the establishment of workhouses.

We rely for most of the information about the Datchworth Green scandal on a pamphlet printed privately by Philip Thicknesse, entitled "An Account of The Four Persons found Starved to Death at Datchworth in Hertfordshire."

Thicknesse was an eccentric character, who had served as Lieutenant Governor of Landguard Fort at Felixstowe for some years. A measure of his peculiarities may be gathered by a clause in his will: "I leave my right hand, to be cut off after my death to my son, Lord Audley, and I desire it may be sent to him in hopes that such a sight may remind him of his duty to God, after having so long abandoned the duty he owed to a father who once affectionately loved him." Nonetheless, there is no reason to doubt his account of what he saw in Datchworth.

"On 23 January 1769," says Thicknesse, "a day labourer, who lately lived in the poor-house belonging to this parish, told me that four or five persons were found dead in a poor-house on the green, and that they perished for want of food, rayment, attendance, and a habitable dwelling." Thicknesse decided to investigate.

He found a small hut, believed to have been located on the opposite end of the Green from the whipping post, "consisting of one room, but without floor or ceiling, 15 feet long and 12 feet broad, unthatched in some places, a window frame without any glass at one end, and on the opposite end a large hole in the plaistering, through which I could have got, and in at which I looked."

Inside were four emaciated bodies, lying on dirty straw. They were James Eaves, his wife and two of his children. "The man had on a piece of shirt, the woman was quite naked, as were the children; nor had they other any other cloaths or covering but the remnant of an old blanket and a sack." This was, remember, in the height of the winter. A third child, a small boy, was crawling around in the straw. He was unable to say how long the rest of the family had been dead.

Right: the bodies of James Eaves and his wife. A detail from the Thicknesse pamphlet.

Thicknesse quizzed the neighbours, and discovered that the family had been ill for some three weeks. Two weeks before, the overseers of the poor had left 2s. 6d. with one of them to buy food for the family. Mrs. Eaves asked the neighbour to buy a faggot (a bundle of twigs or sticks used for fuel), some sugar and a candle, which she did, placing them in the house near the family, together with the change.

No-one checked on them again for eleven days, when a shepherd's boy found them dead. No smoke had been seen from the chimney for two weeks, and the faggot was unused. A rumour had spread that they had the gaol fever (typhus), and it was claimed that no one was prepared to take the risk even to look through the window.

Above: Datchworth Green. The house where the Eaves family died is said to have been to the left side of the picture. (author)

Thicknesse wrote to the churchwarden and the overseer for the poor (John and Samuel Bassett respectively), insisting that the coroner view the bodies before burial.

Believing that the bodies would be swiftly buried nonetheless, Thicknesse went to look at them again. On the way he met the parish constable, driving a cart loaded with the bodies of the Eaves family. The constable assured him that he would comply with Thicknesse's request concerning the coroner viewing the bodies. Actually he was taking them to the rector for burial.

Fortunately Thicknesse also approached the rector, who told him that he (the rector) had been told that the coroner had authorised the burial already. He agreed however to delay the interment until he received written confirmation of the coroner's decision.

Thicknesse suspected a conspiracy, and let it be known that he was going to London. Instead he went to Hatfield to consult with John Searancke, a respected magistrate, whom he believed would be able to help in the matter.

Searancke agreed that if it should prove to be the case that the overseers of the poor had neglected the family, then it was "a crime little short of murder; but I am afraid is not punishable as such."

"A gaoler," he went on to say, "is guilty of wilful murder that suffers a prisoner to die through duress; can an officer of a parish be guilty of a less crime that withholds necessary relief from a pauper?"

When it became know that Thicknesse had "gone to London," the coroner was contacted; he in turn wrote to the parish officers, asking them to summon a jury for the following morning. Thicknesse spoke to the constable, who told him what had happened, and that the churchwarden had instructed him that Thicknesse was not to be part of the jury.

Nonetheless, he was part of the jury; in fact he contrived to be its foreman. His opinion of his fellow jurors was very low. They were, it seems, selected from the "meanest members of the community" - those most likely to reach the desired verdict. They would not accept Thicknesse's argument that there had been any negligence. Finally the coroner pointed out that only two verdicts were open to them: either that the Eaves family had died of natural causes, or that they had been murdered. A verdict of death by natural causes, he said, did not mean that legal proceedings could not be taken at a later date.

Up to this point, the bodies had not been examined by a doctor. At Thicknesse's insistence the inquest was adjourned until the following day, when a surgeon from Hertford, Mr. Frost, came to inspect them. He said that he had never seen bodies so emaciated, and agreed that there was evidence of neglect. He was surprised that no doctor had been called to see the Eaves before their deaths.

One neighbour said that only the boy that survived had been seen in the last few days, when he came to borrow an oven lid. His only clothing had been a sack over his shoulders. She had asked him why he did not go into service; he told her that the parish would not clothe him, and no-one would take him naked.

Mrs. Eaves had been seen about ten days before, going to the pond to fill a kettle, but had fallen, leaving the kettle as she crawled back to the hovel.

It later emerged that another son had visited the Eaves at about Christmas time, and found them "ill and in a starving, helpless condition." He said that they had asked him to "go to the overseer's house and ask for relief; that the overseer was not home, but that a woman there exclaimed, 'Send the relief... Let them die and be damned!' " He went on to say that on his return to inform his distressed parents of his failure to get help for them, he met "the man," who refused to give them any assistance. He told his parents what had happened, and their reply was "then we must perish." He had wanted to pay a further visit, but he was in service, and his mistress would not give him leave to do so.

The survivor from the hut, William Eaves, recovered. Perhaps fortunately, he could recall little of the tragic events.

The overseers, according to Thicknesse, claimed that the Eaves had died of typhus, not malnutrition. A previous occupier of the hut, they said, had died of it in the past. If that were true, Thicknesse asked, why were the family placed in an infected house in the first place?

Several buildings in a community might be used to house the poor, depending upon the demand. Datchworth seems to have had at least two, as the correspondent of the *Ipswich Journal* reported finding another group of paupers in the village housed in circumstances of extreme neglect similar to the Eaves.

Nor it seems were the Eaves the first to die. Susannah Stratton reported that her husband had died in the same poorhouse four years earlier.

At the time it was common for the poor to be "farmed." The task of caring for them was sold to the lowest bidder, whose profit was the difference between what he was paid and the cost of food, clothing and heating for the paupers. Small wonder that in some cases the treatment of the poor left much to be desired. Money was to be made by placing them in huts and sheds rather than in proper housing, as well as by reducing spending on food and clothing to the bare minimum.

Why did the rector apparently not know what was going on? The overall responsibility for the poor of the parish was his. Perhaps he was a trusting soul, who left the matter of the poor in the hands of the appointed officers. Once Thicknesse told him of his fears, he at least agreed not to bury the family until he had written instructions to do so. His sin was probably one of omission.

Why did the neighbours ignore the situation? The rumour of typhus may have frightened some of them, but not that much – remember, one woman lent William Eaves an oven lid, and ask him why he did not enter service. The neighbour who bought the faggot, candle and sugar was not so afraid that she did not enter the hut and leave the items and change there. She must have seen that the family was in a poor way. And Mrs. Eaves was clearly ill when she went to collect water in the kettle; she collapsed on the way back, and left the kettle behind. Yet it seems that none of these people did anything to help. Or perhaps they did; perhaps they contacted the overseers...

In May 1769, the court of the King's Bench moved against the overseers (the Bassetts) concerning their treatment of the poor of the parish. In June, after considering nine affidavits, the court found in their favour. There was, the court said, "not the least reason" to condemn them. It is perhaps not a coincidence that in March the following year neither of the Bassetts was re-elected overseer.

Were the Bassetts responsible for the Eaves' death? I think they must bear the bulk of the blame. At the time, the cost per pauper for a week was considered to be between 1s. 4d. and 2s., and yet they left just 2s. 6d. to keep the whole family for a fortnight. When the son who was in service asked for more help, he was refused. As a result a man, his wife and three children were left without proper clothing, in a hovel with holes in the roof and wall, and with no glass in the window, in the middle of winter.

It is likely that the establishment closed ranks to protect the Bassetts. They were of their own class. One of them was the churchwarden. To permit the action at the King's Bench to succeed would be intolerable. Affidavits in their support were collected and presented, and the case thrown out.

The people of Datchworth Green knew what had happened though, and whether or not the law believed that murder was done, such was the shame that the villagers tried for many years to claim that the events actually took place in another village, Burnham Green.

Thicknesse's pamphlet contains a graphic illustration of conditions in the house. The bodies of the Mr. and Mrs. Eaves lie on a bed of straw, with the youngest child next to them. A second dead child lies beneath a hole in the wall, where Thicknesse first looked in. All are naked except Mrs. Eaves, who wears a cap. All of them resemble inmates of a concentration camp. Amongst the dead, with a rag around his shoulders, sits William, the sole survivor. The proceeds of the sale of the pamphlet were applied to his benefit.

Chapter Five

Walter Clibbon, Footpad and Murderer, Bull's Green, 1782

For some reason a degree of fascination, almost admiration, seems to attach to Walter Clibbon. This is something of a mystery, because he was nothing more than a vicious thief and murderer. He did not even earn the glamour of a highwayman - he was a footpad (what is the difference between a highwayman and a footpad? Answer, a horse). Yet there are two houses in Bull's Green named after him. A post commemorates the spot where he met his end, which was, at least for a time, known as "Old Clibbons."

There are several versions of the story; much of this one is based on the diary of one of the Chief Constables for the Liberty of St. Albans, written at the time the events took place. Other details come from contemporary pamphlets.

Walter Clibbon lived in Babbs Green, Ware, and ran a baker's shop in Hertford. He was married to Elizabeth, and they had at least six children - possibly as many as eleven. The sale of cakes and pies was a front for his more lucrative trade as a robber. He and his sons used it as a cover as they moved through the market looking for likely victims. Who had made a good profit today? It is even said that Elizabeth was involved in more than bakery, though this may be fanciful elaboration. What is sure is that the family as a whole had committed a number of successful robberies over the years.

One of their victims, a Mr. Kent of Bennington, they murdered. They put his body back into his cart, and the horse carried it home, there to be discovered by the unfortunate man's horrified family.

There were suspicions about the Clibbon family, but no proof. No-one had been able to identify them with confidence, as they blackened their faces as a form of disguise.

On Saturday, 28 December 1782 Walter Clibbon, his son Joseph, and an accomplice had lain in wait close to Oaken Valley Bottom, near Bull's Green since morning for a suitable victim. Their patience was at last rewarded when William Whittenbury appeared in his horse and cart. He was robbed, he said, by three men in labourers' smocks, with their faces blackened.

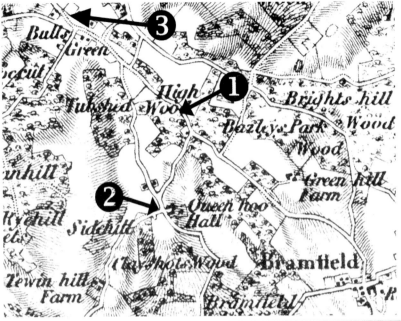

Above: The area of Clibbon's last robbery. 1 – Clibbon's post; 2 – Queen Hoo Hall; 3 – Horns Inn. (courtesy Ordnance Survey). Right: Clibbon's post today. (author)

Prudently, Whittenbury chose not to resist, but went instead to his uncle Benjamin's home at Queen Hoo Hall. Benjamin, his son Thomas, and George North (a servant, known as 'Shock'), set out to track the robbers down. North was armed with a flintlock gun of about .58 inch calibre and 68 inches in length. A dog completed the party. William's father, Robert, and a third Whittenbury brother were known to be on their way home, and it may have been out of concern for their safety that the expedition was so quickly organised.

A short distance down the Bramfield Road out of Bulls Green the group came upon the Clibbon band in the process of robbing the Whittenbury brothers. One had escaped, leaving the other to his fate. Thinking that Benjamin's party were more potential victims from the market, the robbers attacked them too. After a desperate struggle, Walter Clibbon got the better of Benjamin, and sat astride him with a large clasp knife in his hand. Benjamin called, "Shoot, Shock, Shoot, or I am a dead man!"

Shock North fired into Clibbon's body at close range, killing him. One of the assailants ran off, but Joseph Clibbon was caught; he was tried at the Lent Assize at Hertford, found guilty and hanged.

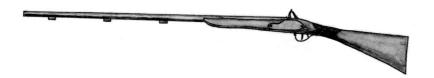

Above: the flintlock sporting gun used by Shock North to kill Walter Clibbon is on display in Hertford Museum. Unfortunately the ramrod and part of the cock are missing. (author)

Walter Clibbon's body was dragged in plough chains to Horns, a nearby public house, where an inquest was held. It is said that the occasion was used as an excuse for considerable drinking, and two (probably untrue) tales of the revels have come down to us.

Jimmy Wilson mixed blood from the corpse with his ginger ale, and with it marked the face of another reveller, causing a fight; and Clibbon's body was dragged by ropes tied to its heels from the outhouse where it had been placed, but rigor mortis had set in; when the heels jammed at the threshold Walter Clibbon reared up as though alive.

Clibbon was buried at the spot where he died, and a commemorative post was erected. The original post has since been replaced.

Benjamin Whittenbury was awarded a 28 oz. silver cup, carrying the following engraving:

> "This cup the gift of James, Earl of Salisbury, Lord Lieutenant, to Mr. Benjamin Whittenbury of Queen Hoo Hall this thirty first day of January 1783 in consideration of his spirited behaviour on Saturday 28 December 1782 in risking his life and securing Joseph Clibbon, the son, after being instrumental in shooting Walter Clibbon, the father a most notorious and inhuman offender, by which means the County of Hertford was delivered from the depredations of a most desperate set of villains."

Above: Horns Inn, where Clibbon's body was dragged following the robbery. (author)

George North was tried for murder, but the verdict was, predictably, justifiable homicide. He was given a long case clock as a reward for his part in the affair.

Whittenbury's cup was sold in 1856, and its whereabouts is unknown. North's clock can be traced to Scotland, but it was stolen in 1972 and is also lost. The gun that North used is now in Hertford Museum, with a fragment of the original post that marked the place where Clibbon died.

A second version of the story was recorded by Francis Lucas, as told to him by an employee of Benjamin Whittenbury in the 1830's. Lucas was writing in the 1870's, so there had been plenty of time for memories to be played false. The essentials of the story are the same but some details vary.

Benjamin Whittenbury was in Hertford that morning, and saw Clibbon watching him. He suspected Clibbon of planning to rob him, and sought out Shock North, his servant, who was also in town, having picked up a gun that had been in for repair.

Whittenbury told North that he was sure he was going to be robbed on the way home. He would leave his money in safe keeping, he said, and take a back road. North he sent on ahead to the place that Whittenbury had identified as the likely location of the robbery. North was to hide behind a tree, and to interfere only if called. Though Whittenbury carried no other weapon than a whip, he was sure that he was a match for Clibbon.

The attack took place just where Whittenbury predicted, but there were two assailants - Clibbon and an accomplice, whose name was Clements.

The struggle was so fierce that Clements fled, leaving Clibbon astride Whittenbury, and feeling for a knife with which to cut his throat. Whittenbury called to North, who shot Clibbon through the body. His corpse was dragged to a local inn for the inquest, after which it was buried at the site of his death. An accomplice was caught, and hanged at the next assizes.

All the Whittenburys except Benjamin (William, Thomas, Robert and the unnamed uncle) have disappeared from this account. The naming of an accomplice as Clements is interesting. Perhaps this was the third man in the earlier version.

Chapter Six

Murder at Hoddesdon, 1807

Thomas Simmons first saw the light of day in 1788, when he was born the son of a shoemaker at Hoddesdon. His father's business was not a great success, however, and he was obliged to abandon it when Thomas was quite young. Thereafter he worked on the land as a ploughman. Sadly he died at an early age, perhaps due to the rigours of his new occupation, when Thomas was just coming into his teenage years.

Thomas went into service with a family of Quaker farmers named Borham. He stayed with them for several years until he reached the age of nineteen, when he was dismissed. He was apparently a foolish young man, who was offensive to other members of the household, and had been suspected of theft on at least one occasion.

Whilst with the Borhams, Thomas had formed a relationship with another of the servants, Elizabeth Harris. She was somewhat older than he was, but they did not see it as a barrier between them.

When he was sacked, however, Elizabeth decided that he was no longer the man for her. In addition, Mrs. Borham disapproved of the match, and an employer's opinion was not to be ignored by a housemaid. The break caused Thomas a good deal of distress: he was deeply attached to Elizabeth, and had hoped to marry her, though he had beaten her before his dismissal, and said that he did not care if he killed her. As far he was concerned Mr. Borham's low opinion of him was the only reason for the break up. He called at the house on several occasions in a drunken state, insisting on speaking to Elizabeth, and making threats against the family.

In 1807 the Borham household consisted of Mr. Borham, his wife, and their three single daughters, Anne, Elizabeth and Sarah. On the evening of 20 October the Borhams were having a pleasant evening at home. Also present was Mrs. Sarah Hummerstone, the housekeeper to Mr. Batty, who kept the Black Lion public house (now the Salisbury Arms), and the Borham's married daughter, Mrs. Esther Warner, the wife of a brass founder.

Thomas Simmons arrived, drunk and swearing. When he saw Elizabeth in the scullery he tried to get into the house. He thrust his hand through the lattice window, just missing the maid with a long-bladed knife he was carrying.

Mrs. Hummerstone heard the commotion. She came through the back of the house into the yard with the intention of telling Simmons to leave the premises. He forced his way past Elizabeth, still brandishing the knife, and before Mrs. Hummerstone could escape, he stabbed her in the throat. He inflicted a second wound, and left her bleeding to death.

The rest of the household were in the parlour. Mr. Borham attempted to stop Simmons with a poker, but the demented young man brushed him aside. Simmons forced his way into the room, his knife dripping blood, and threatened to kill its inhabitants. Without warning he seized Mrs. Warner and stabbed her several times in the throat and breast. She died within moments. The younger women of the company fled to an upstairs room, and locked themselves in.

Mrs. Borham was not so fortunate; Simmons stabbed her in the neck, and then set off after her husband. Elizabeth intervened, and Simmons struck at her too. She managed to wrestle the knife from his grasp, and he turned and fled.

Mr. S. James, a surgeon, arrived, and found Mrs. Hummerstone leaning against a door in the house. She was still alive, but died some three minutes later from a wound in the neck near her spine. Mrs. Warner was already dead. Mrs. Borham, though injured, made a full recovery. Elizabeth had suffered cuts to her hands and arms.

Simmons was found hiding beneath some straw in a crib in the farmyard, "very bloody," and was arrested. He was led to the Bell public house, where he was held overnight. A number of people visited the inn that night in order to look at the murderer. The following morning Mr. Fairfax of the Black Bull found him tightly bound, and relieved the ropes a little before handing him over to the parish constable.

Before the coroner, Benjamin Rook, Simmons declined to make any statement. Rook found that he had murdered the two women, and after an appearance before a magistrate he was remanded to Hertford Gaol, and arraigned to appear before Hertford Assizes in March 1808.

The Borham family, true to their Quaker faith, chose to turn the other cheek, and declined to prosecute Simmons. The community however was not prepared to allow the killer to escape: the Broxbourne vestry minutes contain the following item in November 1807: "It is likewise agreed that the parish officers of the said parish should carry on the prosecution against Thomas Simmons for the wilful murder of Mrs. Esther Warner and Sarah Hummerstone in the hamlet of Hoddesdon on the 20th day of October 1807."

On 4 March 1808 Simmons appeared before Mr. Justice Heath at the Assizes. Amongst the observers in the court was John Carrington, who recorded the event in his diary:

Right: Thomas Simmons in custody in Hertford Gaol, awaiting trial. From a contemporary print.

"Fryday 4 To Hartford againe to the assizes, Simmonds the murder from Hoddesdon I saw Cast & Condemned, as to be Hung on Monday next…"

The evidence was clear and damning. In his summing up, Mr. Justice Heath pointed out to the jury that the accused had several times confessed to the crime; their job was an easy one. It came as no surprise when they found him guilty. The judge sentenced him to be hanged on the following Monday, 8 March.

On the appointed day, before a large crowd, Thomas Simmons was turned off for the cruel and violent acts he had committed a few months before upon two innocent women who had done him no harm. The expenses for the execution were recorded in the Newgate Calendar: horse and cart for conveying the prisoner to place of execution, 10s. 0d.; rope for same and execution, 11s. 6d.; digging grave, 2s. 0d.

Chapter Seven

The Robbery and Murder of William Weare, Elstree, 1823

The murder of William Weare in Elstree excited nationwide interest. What it was about this particular crime that attracted such notoriety is not clear; it seems to have been a rather sordid little affair. Perhaps it was the status of one of the defendants, John Thurtell – he was the son of the mayor of Norwich. Perhaps it was the cold-bloodedness with which the murderers carried out their gruesome task. Public curiosity, then as now, is a fickle thing.

William Weare was a solicitor who liked to gamble. He was good at it, too, and played in company with other professional gamblers to part more gullible enthusiasts from their money.

Thus it was that Weare met John Thurtell in a gambling den in Haymarket, and cheated him of some £300 in a card game called 'blind hookey.'

Thurtell, for all his privileged birth, could ill afford to lose that sort of money. His past had been a catalogue of failure. First the army and the navy, then employment at his father's textile business; his love of gambling, drink and the good life brought nothing but disaster. His debts mounted, and he fled in fear to London, where he and his brother Thomas bought an inn in Watling Street. The premises were destroyed by fire in suspicious circumstances, and the insurance company refused to meet the Thurtells' claim. The brothers took them to court, and won. They invested the money in another inn, the Cock in Haymarket. Thurtell continued in living the high life, and he mixed with some shady characters, amongst them Joseph Hunt.

The manager of the Army and Navy Tavern, Hunt was a fraudster who had served several terms in Newgate. Like Thurtell, he enjoyed high living, and like Thurtell, he too lived beyond his means. His association with the mayor's son was to lead to his downfall.

Following the loss of the £300 to Weare, Thurtell's finances were in desperate straits. Knowing that Weare habitually carried large sums of money on him, he decided that the solution to his problems was to kill and rob the man who had cheated him. With Hunt he planned to invite Weare to Hertfordshire for some shooting. The two men involved another friend of Thurtell, Bill Probert, who lived in Gills Hill Lane, Elstree. The scheme was that Thurtell would bring Weare to Radlett in a gig. At a prearranged place, Hunt would meet them, and together the two men would rob Weare. According to Probert, his role was confined to providing transport and a safe house. Whether he knew that murder was part of the plan no one knows.

Above: the three conspirators - Thurtell, Hunt and Probert, from Pierce Egan's "Account of Trial of John Thurtell and Joseph Hunt," 1824.

Things went wrong from the start. Probert and Hunt, in a horse and cart, were ahead of Thurtell and Weare, and they decided to stop at an inn for a drink, perhaps to raise a little Dutch courage. They calculated that they had plenty of time for Probert to drop Hunt at the chosen spot to wait for his associate and their victim. Probert was to return to Gills Hill Lane and wait for the others there.

Their timing was adrift. While they were drinking, Thurtell and Weare passed the inn on their way to the rendezvous. When they arrived, to Thurtell's consternation Hunt was nowhere to be seen. He drove in circles for a while, until Weare became suspicious. There was nothing for it: Thurtell would have to do the job alone. He drew a pistol and fired at Weare, hitting him in the cheek. Weare staggered from the gig, pleading for mercy and offering to return Thurtell's money. To no avail – Thurtell followed the wounded man, and in the ensuing struggle cut his throat. He rammed his pistol into the side of Weare's head, and into the brain of the dying man. (The gun, a small flintlock, is in the possession of Hertford Museum).

Thurtell dragged the body into the hedge, and took the dead man's purse and money. Now he had his second stroke of ill fortune. He foolishly left his knife and pistol at the scene of the crime.

Meanwhile Probert had taken Hunt to the rendezvous and left him there to await the victim. On his way home he met Thurtell, who told him of the deadly struggle. Probert went back for Hunt, and the three men went to Probert's cottage to decide what to do. When they arrived, Thurtell was foolish enough to allow himself to be seen by a stable boy washing blood from himself.

Above: John Thurtell drives the pistol into William Weare's brain. From a contemporary broadsheet.

Despite Probert's objections, the decision was made to hide the body in his fishpond. They settled down with Mrs. Probert and her sister for a few drinks, and Thurtell gave his hostess Weare's watch chain. On the pretext of organizing some shooting for the following day, the three men left the ladies. But Mrs. Probert knew the company her husband kept, and as she watched from the house she saw the three men lead a horse away into the darkening evening down Gills Hill Lane, and return sometime later with a heavy burden. They carried the weighted body, wrapped in sacking, to the fishpond and threw it in, where it sank to the bottom. Mrs. Probert heard them dividing the haul – according to Thurtell, it came to a disappointing six pounds each. Whether he held some back is open to conjecture. Still anxious about the knife and pistol that had been left behind, the conspirators went to bed.

The following morning Thurtell and Hunt made a disastrous decision. They returned to the murder scene to look for the incriminating evidence. Some workmen saw them, and took an interest in what they were doing, so the two men abandoned their search. The labourers didn't, however, and before long they found the pistol and knife.

Above: The body of William Weare is dumped in Probert's pond. From a contemporary broadsheet.

Thurtell and Hunt fled to London in a panic, but returned to Elstree the following day in an attempt to retrieve the situation. Probert was anxious; he wanted the body out of his pond.   They decided to move it to a less incriminating location. Under cover of darkness they retrieved the dead man, stripped him, wrapped him in sacking once more and carried him off to be buried. But the noise they made caused dogs to bark, and they abandoned the attempt, and threw the body into a muddy pond at Hill Slough, between Elstree and Radlett, again weighed down with heavy stones. The clothes they shredded and scattered in nearby fields.

Meanwhile the labourers had taken the pistol and knife to a Dr. Pidock in Watford. He identified pieces of brain tissue on the pistol. A neighbour of the Proberts had heard tales of their bloodstained visitor, and of the labourers' find. He informed the local magistrates, Robert Clutterbuck and John French, and an investigation began.

Local people testified that they had seen a gig carrying two men in the area, and a Mr. and Mrs. Smith reported hearing a shot. The investigations led to Probert, and when his home was searched Thurtell's bloodstained clothes were found. The stable boy described seeing Thurtell washing off the blood spilt in the course of the murder.

Even then the three men might have escaped justice. The body had not been found; there was nothing to connect them with the knife and the pistol; the only real evidence against them was the testimony of the stable lad. But Bill Probert had had enough. He turned King's evidence, and revealed all he knew of the affair.

The pond where William Weare's body was discovered. From Pierce Egan's "Account of Trial of John Thurtell and Joseph Hunt," 1824.

Hunt and Thurtell were arrested. Thurtell claimed that he was innocent of the charges against him, but Hunt was made of weaker stuff. When some of Weare's possessions were found at his lodgings he quickly broke under questioning, telling the investigators everything. He took them to the pond where the body had been dumped. The corpse was taken to the Artichoke public house at Elstree, where an inquest was held.

Thurtell and Hunt appeared before a packed Hertford Assize Court on 6 January 1824. Hunt pleaded guilty, but John Thurtell denied his involvement, and elected to defend himself.

Murder and Misdemeanour in Hertfordshire

After the evidence was heard, Thurtell made an impassioned, though carefully rehearsed, speech to the jury:

> "Those who know me best know I am utterly incapable of an unjust and dishonourable action, much less of the horrid crime with which I am now charged. There is not, I think, one in this court who does not think me innocent of the charge. If there be, to him or to them I say in the language of the apostle, 'Would to God ye were altogether such as I am, save these bonds.' Gentlemen, I have now done. I look with confidence to your decision. I repose in your hands all that is dear to the gentleman and the man! I have poured my heart before you as to my God! I hope your verdict this day will be such as you may ever after be able to think upon with a composed conscience; and that you will also reflect upon the solemn declaration that I now make – I am innocent! So help me God!"

Above: Thurtell and Hunt appear before Hertford Assizes, January 1824. From a contemporary illustration.

During his summing up, Mr. Justice Parke roundly denounced "the prejudice which has been raised against both prisoners through the press." The newspapers had devoted many columns to the case, most of them presuming the guilt of the accused. Broadsheets were published with the same presumption, and even before the trial began two London theatres put on plays based on the killing. The main attraction was the use as props of as many items as possible actually connected with the crime.

Thurtell's plea of innocence was to no avail. The evidence was damning. Hunt and Probert had both pointed the finger at him; he had been seen in bloodstained clothes; and there was known bad blood between him and Weare following the gaming incident. The jury returned a verdict of guilty, and both Thurtell and Hunt were condemned to death by hanging. Hunt's sentence was commuted to transportation to Australia for life on appeal; in mitigation, he had not actually carried out the murder, and he had pleaded guilty. He eventually became a town mayor, and died in 1861.

Above: the public execution of John Thurtell in front of Hertford Gaol. One of several illustrations of the execution produced at the time.

Thurtell's execution took place on Thursday, 9 January 1824 in front of Hertford Gaol. The crown was enormous, some 15,000 people attending. At noon the condemned man was led to the scaffold. He shook hands with the prison governor and the chaplain, and bowed to friends in the crowd. The hangman, Cheshire, slipped the noose around his neck, and he was "turned off." It is said that the execution was badly managed due to the drunkenness of Cheshire, and that he had to pull on Thurtell's legs several times to end his suffering.

Bill Probert had escaped punishment for his part in the crime by turning King's evidence, but in 1825 he was arrested for horse stealing, and he too died on the scaffold.

Thus ended one of Hertfordshire's most celebrated cases. Despite the mistakes they made, had Probert and Hunt kept their nerve, all three men might have escaped.

As a strange postscript, after the execution a pamphlet entitled "The Hoax Discovered!" was printed. It claimed that William Weare was still alive!

Chapter Eight

"Stortford Flames Shall Reach the Skies..." 1825

On the night of Thursday, 24 March 1825, an attempt was made to destroy by fire the White Horse public house at Bishop's Stortford.

The fire was set in a downstairs room, above which was a loft containing straw and faggots. Fortunately little damage was done, as the fire was discovered before it could take hold. But this was just the beginning of a campaign of arson that so alarmed the town that a reward of £500 was offered for the capture of the culprit – a considerable sum of money in those days.

A few days later, on 4 April, the incendiary struck for a second time. Between eleven and twelve that night, a pile of burning faggots was found in the same room, again being detected early and extinguished.

Perhaps it was the frustration of two failed attempts that caused the culprit to change targets; in any event, the following night he struck at a carpenter's shop in nearby Hockerill with more success. The building was destroyed, as was a barn next door containing corn, the property of Robert Cole.

This spate of fires caused great alarm, and on 6 April the town crier summoned a parish meeting. A committee of eleven local worthies was formed to meet on a daily basis with local magistrates. They organised a subscription for the reward already mentioned, and patrolled the town at night to supplement the town's watchmen.

On the night of 10 April a threatening letter addressed to the committee was left at the post office. It was written on cartridge paper, and ran as follows:

"Revenge is sweet, we defy your police, or your £500. We are strong, – you are weak; if Searle and Dunnage do not come home, Stortford shall be laid in ashes. I am their captain and leader, and we are sworn to revenge. I alone am possessed of a secret to fire any premises at a hundred yards distance, so watch on. There is three of your committee who have made themselves very busy on this occasion, that we have sworn to send to Paradise as soon as possible and stop their piping for the future."

Searle and Dunnage were two Bishop's Stortford men who had been committed to gaol for stealing rabbits. They were eventually sentenced to transportation. The promise to "send to Paradise" the committeemen was a threat to kill them.

The death and arson threats in the letter caused even greater consternation. As there was no county police force, the committee sent for investigating officers from Bow Street. The friends of Searle and Dunnage were questioned, but they did not have the level of literacy required to write such a letter.

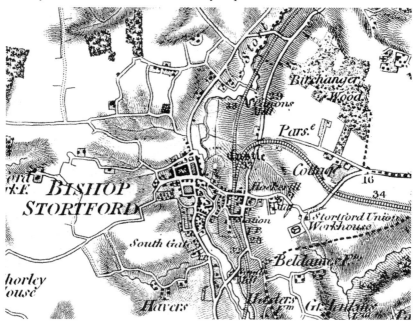

Above: Bishop's Stortford. The survey for this map was carried out in the early 19th century, additions being made over the next 70 years, culminating in the insertion of the railway in 1890. Hockerill is to the east of the town. (courtesy Ordnance Survey).

On 17 April the fire-setter struck again, this time endangering life. William Francis lived in North Street, where he ran a woollen drapery. He had a wife, six daughters, a son and several live-in servants.

At about 4 a.m. the Francis's next-door neighbour, Joseph Bruce, was woken by his daughter, who said, "Father, what a dreadful crackling there is!" Elizabeth Shepperd, one of the Bruces' servants, had also heard the noise, and so loud was it that she thought it was hail on the skylights of the house. Bruce got out of bed and looked out of his window. He could see sparks coming from Francis's woodshed. He pulled on his trousers and ran to raise the alarm, ringing Francis's bell and shouting, "Fire! Fire!" As he did so, he saw Thomas Rees, who lived on the other side of the Francis premises, run from the alley dressed only in his trousers and nightcap.

Sarah Francis heard the bell ringing, and got out of bed. She looked from her window and saw Thomas Rees outside her father's house, waving his arms about most oddly. When she asked him what the matter was, he said, "Your house is afire!" A few moments later Mrs. Francis also saw Rees, by now in the back yard.

Mr. Francis, woken by the bell and the shouting, got out of bed and found that the kitchen and stairs were on fire, and that faggots had also been ignited beneath a beam in the washhouse. He noted a smell of turpentine.

George Bush at the Star Inn also heard and smelt the fire. He too hurried to raise the alarm, and to get the fire engine.

Right: a fire engine from the 1820's. It was drawn and pumped by hand. From an illustration in Firemen and their Exploits, *published in 1899.*

Once the flames had been subdued, an investigation began. It was a joint effort between the Bow Street officer, J. J. Smith, and members of the committee set up to counter the menace.

They found that the arsonist had broken open a window into the Francis house and carried in faggots from the outhouse. Wheat straw had been used to get the fire going, and remaining fragments smelled strongly of turpentine or rosin, presumably used as an accelerant. The fire in the washhouse had been started on a stool beneath a wooden beam, but had gone out before the alarm was raised, though the beam was much scorched. On the floor lay some pieces of blackened glass, with the remains of gilded lettering on the back.

The fire beneath the stairs had been started in a cupboard, and though the faggots were burned and the surrounding woodwork damaged, the flames had failed to take hold there either; probably due to lack of oxygen, being sealed in the cupboard. Thus it was only by sheer incompetence on the part of the arsonist that the fire did not spread, with the considerable risk to life that might have resulted.

In addition to the fire, there had been a theft. From the kitchen, four silver spoons were missing.

The layout of the premises led the investigators to believe that the perpetrator must have got in from one of the adjoining properties. To the north was William Rees, a shoemaker; to the south lived Joseph Bruce, a druggist. To the east was the stable of the Star Inn, surrounded by a brick wall about eight feet high, topped with a wooden fence with iron spikes on top - about ten feet high altogether.

Against the northern corner of this wall was placed a ladder, taken from Mr. Francis's outhouse. The consensus of opinion was that it was a red herring that had been placed there by the arsonist to throw the investigators off the scent. The investigators came to this conclusion for two reasons: firstly, there were no indentations in the ground at the foot of the ladder, as might be expected if it had borne the weight of a man; and secondly, there were no marks or damage to the fence or the spikes at the top.

In the Rees's yard there was a shed, built onto the boundary fence between them and the Francis yard. Inside was a partition of loose boards, which could easily have been moved to allow access between the two properties. Also in the shed was a large tub of rosin.

During the search of the Rees property, fragments of glass similar to that found in the washhouse came to light; and small quantities of wheat straw were found, as were fragments of wheat ears between the two households. The Bruce family had only barley straw on their premises.

The search was thorough – it extended to the contents of the privy, lying upon the malodorous surface of which was found a matchbox.

Elizabeth Shepperd had one more interesting tale to tell. At between 10 and 11 that night she had been walking from her master's house to his warehouse when she saw William Rees' son Thomas with a ladder, dressed in nothing but his shirt. When he saw her, he said, "Betsey, I want a bedfellow." "Then you must get one," replied Eliza, rather sharply.

During the evening of 18 April John Turner, a servant to Mr. Gee, a solicitor, found a second letter near the chancel of the church:

"Devils, tremble: this is only the beginning: before one week is at an end you shall see such things as were never yet seen in Stortford.

Devils, believe and tremble; dare you reject our proffered peace! dare you reject our mercy! woe be to three of Stortford!
Pray send that lurcher home to his kennel in the lower hells on the back slums: £500 shall never bribe one of us to open our mouths, except it is to chaunt forth – Fire! fire! fire!
Stortford flames shall reach the skies.

N.B. Read, mark, believe, and tremble."

The reference to the lurcher was taken to mean the Bow Street officer. The rest spoke for itself. After passing through the hands of several intermediaries, the letter reached Mr. Gee.

The investigators believed that they had enough evidence to arrest Thomas Rees, and he was taken into custody on charges of arson, burglary and issuing threatening letters. He was arraigned to appear before Hertford Summer Assizes, and remanded to Hertford Gaol.

In July Thomas Rees appeared before Mr. Baron Graham to answer the charges. He was respectably dressed in a green frock coat with a velvet collar, light trousers, and a striped waistcoat. He wore a white cravat, fixed with a large brooch. Between twenty-four and twenty-five years of age, he was about 5' 7" tall, with a sallow complexion, dark eyes and a Roman nose.

Messrs. Andrews, Broderick and Adolphus appeared for the prosecution; Messrs. Jessop, Price and Law for the defence.

Mr. Andrews addressed the jury, informing them that in the event of a conviction, Thomas Rees was likely to hang. They should dismiss this from their minds, and concentrate upon the facts laid before them. He outlined the case for the prosecution, detailing the catalogue of fires, the letters, the layout of the buildings, and the evidence already described. In addition, Rees had been seen in the vicinity of the churchyard when the second letter had been found.

He went on to tell them that Thomas Rees had, on 6 June, whilst in Hertford Gaol, confessed his guilt to a fellow prisoner, Francis Anderson. The two men had subsequently argued, and Anderson had gone to the Prison Governor and told him of the confession. Rees had approached another prisoner by the name of Carter and asked him to say that Anderson was lying; if he did so, Rees had told him that when they were free he would treat him (Carter) to a "good spree." Carter had declined the offer.

Andrews then called his witnesses, including James Bush and John Fowler, both of whom said that Rees had told them the contents of the first letter before it became general knowledge. This evidence was partially undermined by Thomas Ley, Mr. Gee's Clerk, who admitted that he had discussed the letter with Thomas' father; he could not say whether Thomas may have overheard.

J. H. Mullinger, a stationer, and his assistant, James Large, testified that Thomas Rees had bought cartridge paper, but this proved little, as such paper was regularly used by shoemakers to produce patterns.

Such was the case for the prosecution. The judge summed up in detail, and sent the jury to their deliberations. In ten minutes they returned a verdict of not guilty of arson.

Rees was then arraigned on the charge of burglary, but was acquitted when no evidence was offered.

On the third charge of sending threatening letters Thomas Rees was found guilty. The judge pronounced sentence: transportation for life.

Did Thomas Rees set the four fires with which he was charged? It may be significant that the most concerted attempt at arson was carried out against his next-door neighbour. Did he hold a grudge against a member of the Francis family, or one of their servants? Perhaps the other fires and the letters were a smokescreen to divert suspicion from the true target of his wrath.

Perhaps too the jury thought him guilty, but after Mr. Andrews' remarks regarding an almost certain capital sentence, chose to find him guilty only of the lesser charge of sending threatening letters. Regrettably, in this case, the truth will remain a mystery. It is worthy of note however that the spate of fires stopped following Thomas's arrest.

It is also worth remembering that whoever lit that last fire in the home of William Francis, he or she endangered the life of Francis himself, his wife, their children, and their servants too.

Chapter Nine

John Tawell's Secret, Berkhamsted, 1845

In the 19th century, Mechanics' Institutes sprang up in towns all over the country. The purpose was to better the education of the working man by providing evening classes, lectures and access to libraries.

Berkhamsted was no exception, though there were those who thought that the establishment of an institute in the town was doomed to failure. Berkhamsted was "a soil on which a Mechanics' Institute cannot live and flourish." There had been difficulty enough in establishing schools in the town - what were the chances of adult education succeeding?

Amongst the supporters of the establishment of an institute was John Tawell, a wealthy man in his early sixties. He was involved in many local civic projects. It was therefore no surprise that, when a vote was taken, he was nominated as part of a committee of five leading citizens formed to consider how an institute might be organized. An initial meeting was held at Tawell's house. He lived almost opposite the church with his second wife in considerable comfort, cared for by six servants. At this preliminary meeting initial duties were assigned, and a date was set for a second gathering.

Before it could take place, the rumour flew about the town that a woman named Sarah Hart had been poisoned near Slough, in Berkshire, and that John Tawell had been arrested for her murder. The people of Berkhamsted were astonished; surely it could not be true. None could have been more shocked than Mrs. Tawell, however; the first inkling she had of the affair was from the newspaper reports. Her own husband, arrested for murde r...

The people of Berkhamsted did not know that the man who had become one of their most respected citizens was a convicted criminal and an adulterer. Had they done so, they might been less surprised by his arrest.

Tawell had been a member of the Quaker Society of Friends when, some years before, he had been found guilty of forgery, and sentenced to transportation for 21 years. The forgery had been substantial - a thousand pounds, and committed against one of the partners of the Uxbridge Bank. Tawell's good conduct in Australia earned him a ticket of leave after only seven years, and he set up in business in Sydney as a chemist and druggist. He also became involved in the shipping trade. In this manner he made a substantial fortune, and returned to England.

He had lived in Berkhamsted for about four years, and married a local widow, Mrs. Cutforth, who kept a ladies' school in the town. A daughter of his first marriage lived with them; there had been two sons, but they had both died. In addition there was a ten-month old child from this second union.

Sarah Hart had been a servant at Tawell's home both before and after the death of his first wife. Indeed, she was more than a servant - she had every expectation of becoming the second Mrs. Tawell.

Shortly before his marriage to Mrs. Cutforth, Tawell induced Sarah to move out of his home and into a succession of lodgings, finally ending up at Salt Hill, now a district of Slough to the west of the town centre. Tawell gave her an allowance of £13 per quarter, and visited her regularly. For her part, she told neighbours that she was married to Tawell's son. She said that her two children were by him, and that he was living overseas. Mr. Tawell senior came to see her, she said, to pay her an allowance, though he disapproved of their match. In reality, of course, the children were Tawell's.

In September 1844 Tawell visited Sarah, and brought with him a bottle of Guinness stout. Shortly afterwards, she was taken violently ill, but made a full recovery.

On the morning of 1 January 1845, Tawell bought prussic acid from a Mr. Thomas. It was not the first time. The reason he gave was that he needed it to treat his varicose veins.

At 4.00 p.m., dressed in Quaker garb, Tawell caught the Great Western Railway train for Slough. He must have arrived at Sarah's home at between 4.30 and 5.00 p.m. Mary Ashley, who lived next door, was a little vague - somewhere between 4 and 5, she said.

Somewhere between 1½ - 2 hours later, Mary heard a stifled scream. Thinking that her neighbour had been taken ill, she took a candle and went next door. She met Tawell near the gate. He seemed in an agitated state, and she opened the gate for him. As she neared the entrance to the house she looked back and found him staring at her in such a manner as to cause her to hurry inside, closing and fastening the door behind her.

She found Sarah lying near to the door, her clothing disordered, with her petticoats up almost to her knees and one stocking torn and a shoe missing. She was making a noise, and her eyes were fixed. She was frothing at the corners of the mouth. Mary called for assistance, and a surgeon, Mr. Henry Champneys, attended. He bled Sarah, but she was found already to be dead.

On the table, Mary noticed two glasses. One was empty but for a little froth, the other half full of stout or porter. Evidence was later presented that Tawell had bought another bottle of Guinness that evening.

Meanwhile, a post-boy had seen Tawell running from the house. He caught an omnibus towards Eton, perhaps in order to kill time until the next Paddington train, which was not due until 7.42 p.m. Several witnesses saw a man in Quaker garb, but were unable to identify him with any certainty.

A local parson, the Reverend E. T. Champnes, had heard of the suspicious death, and of a man in Quaker clothing running away. He went to the railway station, where he saw Tawell board the train. At the parson's instigation, the station superintendent sent an electric telegraph message to Paddington, giving a full description of the suspect.

The use of the telegraph to warn Paddington that a suspected killer was on the train was the first example of its use for such a purpose. The system of code at the time had only twenty letters, one of those omitted being 'Q' - Morse code was yet to be developed. The word 'Quaker' had therefore to be spelt 'Kwaker,' which caused some confusion at Paddington; fortunately it was eventually realised that the spelling was phonetic.

At about 8.30 p.m. Sergeant William Williams of the Railway Police spotted Tawell at Paddington, and followed him via a number of ports of call to Mr. Hughes' lodging house at no. 7, Scott's Yard.

The following morning, Tawell was taken into custody at the Jerusalem Coffee House. Initially he denied having been in Slough the previous evening, or knowing anyone that lived there; later he modified his story considerably.

Tawell's final version of events was as follows: Sarah had been a servant in his home for about 2½ years, but had left about five years before. At this point he was cautioned that anything he said might be reported to the Coroner. Undeterred, he went on to say that Sarah had pestered him for money over the years; and that she had been a good servant, but was "a very bad-principled woman." He visited her on 1 January to tell her that there would be no more money. She asked him for some porter, and he had sent out for some Guinness. When it was poured, he claimed, she had held her hand over her glass, and said "I will, I will," emptying the contents of a small phiall into it. She had drunk some of the contents, thrown the rest into the fire, and fallen into convulsions. He thought that she was play-acting, he said, and left the house.

Much of the testimony above appeared at the inquest, along with Mr. Champneys' statement that he had performed an autopsy on Sarah's body. He had collected her stomach contents and tested them for a number of possible toxins. He had found prussic acid. (Prussic, or hydrocyanic acid, is a cyanide-based poison. Taken in any quantity it results in paralysis of the heart and lungs). Champneys could find no trace of that substance in either of the glasses on the table however.

The jury recorded a verdict of "Wilful Murder against John Tawell, for poisoning Sarah Hart with prussic acid." He was remanded in custody pending his trial.

The trial was held in Aylesbury, before Baron Parke. Tawell engaged a first class legal team - his costs were greater than those of the prosecution by some £300.

There was no doubt that Tawell had had the opportunity to kill Sarah. His strange behaviour at the gate of Sarah's house had not been that of an innocent man. He had lied to the police. He had bought prussic acid. If his story of Sarah killing herself had been true, why had he not told the police at once, rather than lie to them?

But it was all circumstantial evidence. No one saw Tawell administer the poison. Nonetheless, said Baron Parke in his summing up to the jury, if circumstantial evidence is compelling enough that there can be no rational doubt, then it is enough to convict.

Tawell may have spent a small fortune on his defence team, but they were fighting a losing battle from the start. The jury took only half an hour to find John Tawell guilty of the murder of Sarah Hart.

The judge was scathing in his condemnation. Sarah had accepted the drink believing Tawell was her friend and protector. Tawell's life was marked by hypocrisy, during which he had adopted the garb of a peaceful and religious man. He was to hang, and his body buried within the confines of the prison. "And may God have mercy on your miserable soul."

On the morning of Friday, 28 March 1845, in front of Aylesbury Town Hall and before a crowd of some 5,000 people, John Tawell was hanged by William Calcraft, the executioner. The cap was placed over his head; for about a minute and a half he knelt to pray. After a slight delay, which raised a murmur in the crowd, the rope was placed around his neck and the trap fell. His body convulsed violently, his arms and legs contracting three times. He was left to hang for an hour, before being taken down and returned to Aylesbury Gaol for burial.

In his last hours, John Tawell confessed to his crime. He also confessed to having tried to kill Sarah the previous September. And at last his motive was revealed: he did not want his wife to find out about the affair he had been having with his ex-servant girl.

To her enduring credit, the second Mrs. Tawell, when she discovered that no provision had been made for Sarah's two children, a girl and a boy, aged four and five, indicated that she would make some payment towards securing their future; the only act of decency in the whole sorry tale.

John Tawell's Secret

Above: The newspapers had a field day with the conviction of John Tawell, especially as he seemed a thoroughly respectable individual.

Chapter Ten

The Murder of Constable Starkins Norton Green, Stevenage 1857

Hertfordshire County Constabulary was formed in April 1841 under the County Police Act of 1839. The act was an enabling act - that is, it allowed counties to form police forces, but did not force them to do so; compulsion followed in 1856, a year or so before the events described in this chapter took place.

The debate of 1839-40 in Hertfordshire was a bitter one, with opinions strongly held on both sides. People in rural areas believed that they would be subsidizing the urban areas, and that they would receive little benefit from the new force. The number of constables proposed was so few, they thought, that the force could not possibly cover the countryside adequately. The townsfolk tended towards the opposite view, that a police force was essential for the maintenance of law and order. In the event, the new force rapidly became popular with the great majority, both town and country.

It was not until sixteen years later, in 1857, that the force suffered its first loss at the hands of a murderer, and the news came as a shock.

Constable John Starkins came from St. Albans, and was about 25 years old. For some years he had worked for the Earl of Verulam, but had left to join the police force a few months before. From the 17 September he had been stationed at Stevenage, then little more than a village.

On 21 October Starkins received instructions from Inspector Hawkes to keep an eye on Jeremiah Carpenter. Hawkes suspected Carpenter of stealing corn from his employer, Mr. Edward Horn of Norton Green Farm, which was not far from the six burial mounds still visible near Six Hills Way in the new town. If Starkins saw Carpenter, he was to stop and search him, a not uncommon practice at that time.

Hawkes last saw Starkins on 30 October at about 1 p.m., when he gave the constable instructions to patrol in the area of Norton Green, though he did not at that time repeat his instructions to watch for Carpenter. Starkins was due to report back to the inspector that evening at 9 p.m. When he did not appear, Hawkes visited the house of Mrs. Pamela Barry in Stevenage where the constable lodged. Mrs. Barry told him that she had not seen Constable Starkins since 5 p.m. There was little to be done that night, but the following morning Hawkes called again, and found that the constable had still not come home.

The inspector was now worried. Over the weekend he and the other Stevenage officers searched for the missing man, enlisting the aid of volunteers with dogs. They failed to find him, and on Monday 2 November officers from Hitchin under the command of Inspector Capron were drafted in to help.

Amongst those aiding the search was Constable William Isgate, and it was he who at about 11 a.m. made a gruesome discovery in a field known as Cooper's Braches. The field was partly stubble and partly planted with turnips. At one end there was a pond. Isgate saw a foot protruding from the water, and below the surface he could make out the shape of a human hand.

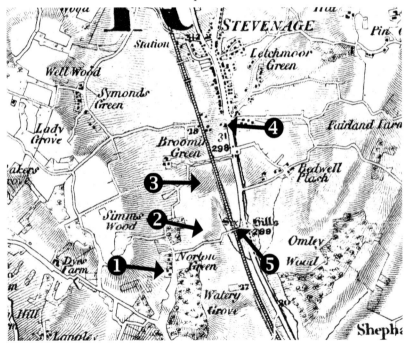

Above: the area of Stevenage and Norton Green. 1. Norton Green Farm; 2. Railway Field, where Carpenter was working on the day of the murder; 3. Cooper's Braches, where the body was found; 4. Carpenter's cottage; 5. Six Hills railway bridge, where Starkins was seen at 5:20 p.m. (courtesy Ordnance Survey).

Inspectors Hawkes and Capron were in the next field, and Isgate called them over. He and Constable Wilson pulled the dead man from the pool. His throat had been dreadfully cut, and his head almost severed from his body. The officers sent for George Smith, a Fellow of the Royal College of Surgeons, to examine the body and certify death, after which arrangements were made to take Constable Starkins to the Chequers Public House in Stevenage. There they searched his pockets. They found his memorandum book, seven shillings in silver, two police buttons, a handcuff key, and a second, unidentified, key. Robbery was clearly not the motive for the crime.

The officers began their investigation into the brutal murder of their colleague. They organized a search of the Braches, and began tracing the movements of both Starkins and the obvious suspect – Jeremiah Carpenter. It was he that Starkins had been told to watch.

Both lines of investigation quickly yielded results. About twenty yards from the pond they found that the grass was trampled down, as if a scuffle had taken place. A good deal of blood had been spilled upon the grass – Hawkes estimated several pints. From there to the water were the marks of something heavy having been dragged. At the edge of the pool there were footmarks, and the soil was disturbed.

Nearby, almost hidden in the long grass, was the stick that Starkins had carried with him. Almost a hundred yards away, near the boundary of the field, were more signs of men struggling. Some wheat and barley grains lay there amongst the stubble. Constable George Killey found Starkins' handcuffs some thirty yards from the pond, between the two places where the signs of the scuffles had been discovered. They were open, suggesting that the constable had been about to use them. Several turnips in the field had been freshly uprooted, and lay on the ground.

Inspector Hawkes had already visited Carpenter on the day after his man had gone missing. He found the labourer nursing an injured leg, which he got, he said, when a tree root had fallen on him from his woodpile the previous evening. In answer to Hawkes' questions, Carpenter said that he had got home from work the night before at about 5:30 p.m. He had not taken the direct route home, but had gone via Gunwell's Wood (now covered by Gunnels Wood Road), and past two cottages which stood in the field nearby.

After Starkins' body was found Hawkes went back to see Carpenter, and asked him for his knife. Mrs. Carpenter had lent it to their son, David, and it was from him that the blade was recovered later that day. Hawkes also examined some of Carpenter's clothing, and found marks that he thought were bloodstains. Meanwhile, other officers were questioning local people to trace Starkins' and Carpenter's movements on the evening of the murder. They wanted to break their suspect's story. It seemed it wouldn't be hard to do so.

Starkins' landlady, Pamela Barry, said that he had been carrying his stick and handcuffs when he left home at 5 p.m. Thomas Cooper saw a policeman he thought was Starkins crossing the railway bridge near Six Hills at 5:25 p.m. A few minutes later, Emma Poterow and Elizabeth Roe, both of whom lived on Wilmer Common, saw a policeman in the area of the Braches, looking over the hedge. Emma was sure it was a policeman she saw, because he wore a shiny black top hat. They saw no one else in the area at that time.

Carpenter lived in one of four cottages a few hundred yards to the south of Stevenage, and about a mile from Norton Green Farm. On the day in question, he said, he had been working in Railway Field between the farm and his home, about twenty or twenty-five minutes' leisurely walk away. According to William Shepherd, Carpenter's next-door-but-one neighbour, the suspected man did not get home until 6:10 p.m. Shepherd was surprised to see his workmate coming home so late, because he too worked at Norton Green Farm, and had left late himself, having been delayed at the farm. The most direct route home from Railway Field was across Cooper's Braches, and it was from this direction that Shepherd said he saw Carpenter coming home.

Above: the farmhouse at Norton Green Farm, where both Carpenter and Shepherd worked. (author)

A few minutes later, Mrs. Carpenter called to Shepherd for help. Her husband had been splitting wood in the yard, and a large tree root had fallen from the stack onto his leg, pinning him to the ground. Shepherd at once went to assist the injured man, removing the wood and helping him indoors. Shepherd noticed that Carpenter had changed from his working smock into his dark green Sunday garment; he explained this by saying that he had been intending to walk into Stevenage to buy some pork victuals. Shepherd was also surprised to find that Carpenter's leg was already swollen, though the accident had happened only minutes before. The injury was sufficiently serious that, though Carpenter went to work the next morning, still in his Sunday smock, he was forced to return home as unfit for work. He was unable to work on Sunday or Monday either.

William Shepherd junior, only nine years old, had an explanation for the sudden swelling of Carpenter's leg: he had noticed that the man was limping when he arrived home. The injury must therefore have been caused some time before the woodpile incident. He was told by Mrs. Carpenter to say nothing. His father too told him to keep quiet, or get a beating, but he spoke up, nonetheless.

The police interviewed the inhabitants of the two cottages that Carpenter had claimed he had passed on his way home. They swore that, had he done so, then they would have seen him. They had not.

William Red, foreman of Norton Green Farm, told the officers that on 29 October, the day before Starkins disappeared, Carpenter had been sowing red wheat mixed with a little barley. Indeed, he had been sent back to the farm to get a further supply of grain, as it looked as though the men would run out before the field was finished.

The police were now sure that they had their man. They had witnesses putting John Starkins only 150 yards from Coopers Braches just after 5:30 p.m. No one else was seen in the area. The constable had been instructed to watch for Carpenter as a suspected thief. Other witnesses' testimony indicated that Carpenter was lying about both his route home and the time he got there. There were at least twenty minutes missing in the suspected man's account of that evening's events. Carpenter had had an injured leg when he got home, an injury that he had tried to cover up with a bogus accident.

The police believed that the real course of events ran as follows: on Thursday 29 October Carpenter had hidden some of the grain he had been sent to fetch from the farm, planning to pick it up the next day. He had indeed collected it, and was in the process of stealing turnips too when he saw Constable Starkins. Carpenter dropped the turnips, but Starkins still stopped him and insisted on searching his basket. There was a struggle, during which some of the stolen grain was spilled. Carpenter got away, but Starkins chased him, getting his handcuffs ready to restrain the man. There was a second struggle, during which the constable's throat was cut. At some stage Carpenter received a blow to his leg, perhaps from a kick, or possibly from the officer's stick.

Carpenter dragged the constable's body to the pond, and rolled him in. Starkins' stick he threw into the field. He then limped home, changed his bloodstained smock, and concocted the story of the falling timber to account for his injury.

It was a plausible theory, though the evidence was circumstantial. Nonetheless, on 3 November Superintendent Barnes arrested Jeremiah Carpenter and charged him with the wilful murder of John Starkins. The police also suspected that Shepherd knew more than he was saying – perhaps the two men had both been stealing from their employer. Meanwhile, a reward of £50 was offered for information leading to the conviction of the murderer or murderers, in case others were involved.

The press reaction to the murder was instantly hostile to the accused man. The Hertford Mercury, for example, said that "The evidence against [Carpenter] is so conclusive that there cannot be the slightest doubt as to his being the party, or one of the parties, guilty of this atrocious deed."

The inquest was opened on the same day that Barnes arrested Carpenter. The coroner and the jury heard from several witnesses, for the most part officers involved in the finding of the body. The hearing was adjourned to allow a post mortem to be carried out.

The investigation continued. A search of Carpenter's cottage revealed a much cut-about smock. The sleeves had been torn out, and a panel removed from the front. The police later managed to recover some of the missing fragments of the garment, and they found what they believed to be bloodstains. Mrs. Carpenter was not in the least cooperative with the search. These fragments, along with a section of Carpenter's basket, his clothes, boots, gaiters and knife were sent for examination by Professor Taylor, a forensic scientist at Guy's Hospital in London.

Barnes had already found grains of wheat and barley, similar to those found close to the crime scene, amongst the weave of the basket.

On 10 November Carpenter appeared before the Stevenage magistrates. Much of the evidence already detailed was presented to them. Additionally, they heard the sworn statement of Professor Taylor, offering his findings on the examination of the items sent to him. The knife had looked clean, but the professor had removed the handle, beneath which he found coagulated blood. The smock had no identifiable bloodstains, and the trousers only had a small quantity on one of the buttons and some of the sewing. The boots were free of blood, but the professor found more on the gaiters, especially on the left side. The shirt displayed numerous bloodspots. The left wristband was stiffened. Carpenter claimed this was caused by the lead acetate ointment he had been putting on his leg, but it was not: it was a mixture of soap and blue vitriol. The basket had bloodstains on it. At the end of the hearing, Captain

Robertson asked that young William Shepherd be placed in the custody of the wife of one of his constables, for fear that he might be intimidated by his father or Mrs. Carpenter. With some reluctance, the magistrates agreed. They remanded Carpenter in custody for a week.

On the same day as the magistrates' hearing the inquest resumed, and heard the results of the post mortem, and the testimony of some of the witnesses that appeared at the magistrates' court. They were shown the knife, and Starkins' coat. The knife was a clasp knife with a buckhorn handle. The blade was 3½ inches long, with a serrated edge and a blunt point. The coat showed signs of damage to the collar matching the knife. Once more the court adjourned.

The police were still collecting evidence. At the edge of Gunwell's Wood, Inspector Evans' attention was drawn by Isaac Norman, a labourer, to a quantity of grain hidden beneath a pile of grass and leaves. It was similar to the other samples of grain – a mixture of wheat and barley. A pearl button from a pair of gaiters also came to light. Some of the buttons on Carpenter's gaiters were of the same design; others were missing.

On Monday 19 November the inquest resumed for the second time, and the new evidence was laid before the court. The Coroner summed up the evidence for the jury, which, after half an hour's consideration, returned a verdict of wilful murder against Carpenter.

On the morning of 21 November the accused man appeared before the magistrates once more. Very little new evidence was presented, but the Bench was sufficiently convinced by what they heard to commit Carpenter to Hertford Gaol to appear before the next Assizes.

The trial began on Friday, 5 March 1858 before Mr. Justice Williams. Mr. Hawkins and Mr. Pollock appeared for the prosecution, and Mr. Sergeant Parry and Mr. Watkin Williams for the defence.

Mr. Hawkins addressed the jury at length, pointing out the important locations on a plan. He described the prosecution's version of events, and the evidence that he would be presenting to them. He finished his speech with something of a bombshell: as Carpenter was being transported in the prison van on 3 March, he had been overheard in conversation with a fellow prisoner. In the course of the exchange Carpenter had admitted killing Starkins. The conversation had been overheard by Constable William Quint, who was, unknown to the two prisoners, in another part of the van.

George Smith and George Dunn took the stand and gave medical evidence. Constable Starkins' throat had been deeply cut, right back to the spine. The collar of the policeman's coat had also been cut in the attack. The wound, which was more than four inches long, parted the carotid arteries and all the blood vessels. The constable's head had been almost severed from his body. Both doctors agreed that the injury was inflicted with a good deal of force, and that the knife used was probably not very sharp. The blade had pushed aside some of the cartilage that a sharper knife would have cut through; and the edges of the wound were serrated. Death would have followed in about one minute.

Carpenter gave two explanations for the blood on his clothing. He had been helping put rings in pigs' noses the week before the body was found; and he suffered from regular nosebleeds. Edward Horn, his employer, and William Red, the farm foreman, confirmed his story, as did William Shepherd, who said that he had seen Carpenter's nose bleed three or four times in one day.

George Smith, the surgeon, was recalled, and asked to comment on the state of the injury to Carpenter's leg. Was it consistent with having been caused by a falling piece of timber? Smith thought that it was. The prosecution case, which had looked so strong, was beginning to falter.

Professor Taylor told the court that it was not possible to say that the bloodstains found were human, and that fleabites could explain the blood spots on the shirt. The bloodstains on the basket could have resulted from its being used to transport meat.

Everything hung in the balance as Constable William Quint took the stand. He told the court that he had been detailed to escort prisoners between the gaol and the court in the prison van on the previous Wednesday, and he had been in the van in which Carpenter and another prisoner, later identified as Henry Ringshall, had been locked in their separate cells. The prisoners had been unable to see Quint. The van was wheeled into the street, where it stopped for about five minutes. During that time, said Quint, the following conversation took place:

Carpenter: What did you get?
Ringshall: Ten months.
Carpenter: I have not had my trial.
Ringshall: What are you in for?
Carpenter: For the murder of Starkins.

The van then moved on to the prison gates, where it stopped. The conversation resumed.

Carpenter: Do you know whether Shepherd said anything?
Ringshall: No.
Carpenter: If he has, he will do me.
Ringshall: Do they know who done it?
Carpenter: No, I done it, but nobody knows it.

Quint said that he did not know who the second prisoner was - no one had asked him to point the man out. As Sergeant Parry cross-examined him, Quint collapsed in the witness box. His coat and collar were loosened, but he did not regain consciousness, and was carried out of the court. As the constable showed no signs of an immediate recovery, and as it was getting late, the court adjourned for the day.

At 9 a.m. the following morning the court resumed, and Constable Quint returned to the witness box. He told the court that there had been two other prisoners in the van; apart from the driver, the only other person present was a small girl, who he thought might be the daughter of one of the turnkeys. As soon as the van had arrived at the prison, Quint had told one of the gaolers about the conversation.

The prosecution asked the constable one or two more questions, from which it emerged that the previous day he had been on duty since 8:30 a.m. until called as a witness in the early evening. In that time he had had nothing to eat, which might explain his collapse.

Above: a prison van, similar to that in use in Hertford in 1858.

After Quint was dismissed, a member of the jury asked if Ringshall would be testifying. After a brief discussion the judge agreed, but warned the jury that the man was a convicted felon, and that they must bear that in mind when considering what he said. Ringshall duly took the stand, and admitted that he had spoken to Carpenter. He said however that the conversation was far shorter than Quint's version. Carpenter had asked him what his sentence was, and Ringshall had told him. Nothing further passed between the two men.

The jury now requested that the small girl who had been in the van be called. Her name was Mary Ann Dunning, and she was indeed the daughter of one of the gaolers. On the trip in question she said that she had sat on a box next to the driver, but inside the van. She had heard some conversation as the van went down Fore Street, but had not been able to make out the words. She heard nothing while the van was stationary.

Mary Ann's father, Stephen Dunning, was the next witness. As far as he remembered, Carpenter and Ringshall had not been in adjacent cells – a prisoner called Maltby had been between them. The only conversation he had heard was at the prison gate, though he might not have heard words exchanged while the van was in motion. At the prison he had stopped the prisoners conversing straight away. No more than a few words had been said. Dunning also denied that the van had been motionless outside the court, as Quint had claimed.

Mr. Hatchard, the prison governor, explained the layout of the prison van. There were seven compartments. The police officer's station had a separate entrance; the others were arranged, three each side, along a central corridor. The doors were close fitting, and there were no bars. Ventilation was provided by an aperture in the roof of each cell. The jury was taken to look at the van, which was outside the court. They found by experimentation that a person in the officer's seat could hear a whisper uttered in the cells.

There were thus four versions of the journey of the prison van, and all of them contradictory in one or more respects. The credibility of Constable Quint was seriously damaged. There were some who went so far as to suggest that he had fainted because of a guilty conscience, or even that it was a judgment of God.

With this inspection, the presentation of evidence and testimony was complete, and Sergeant Parry began his address to the jury.

The case against Carpenter was, he maintained, circumstantial. Circumstantial evidence was often valuable, but only when it formed a complete picture, and one that was open to no other interpretation but that the accused was guilty. There was no direct evidence that Carpenter had met with and killed Starkins. Parry went through the main points of the evidence.

The wheat and barley grains found in the wood may not have been from Norton Green, but even if they were, there were others with access to it – there was nothing to connect it to Carpenter. The grains in Carpenter's basket proved nothing either – indeed, it would be surprising if there were none in the basket of an agricultural labourer. There were discrepancies in the times that various witnesses claimed to have seen Starkins and Carpenter. The two struggles in Cooper's Braches, the pursuit, the murder, and the disposal of the body must have taken some time. But a witness had stated that she had seen Starkins almost 400 yards from the field at 5:45 p.m. How could Carpenter have done all he was accused of and still get home just after 6 p.m., especially with an injury to his leg?

The occupants of the two cottages that Carpenter said he passed on his way home that night had, by their own admission, been in and out of their houses – he may well have passed them without being seen, suggested Parry.

Parry next attacked the claim by the prosecution that Carpenter had faked the woodpile accident to explain an injury that he had received during the murder. Carpenter was an ignorant labourer - was it likely that he would invent such an ingenious scheme? Shepherd confirmed that the accident had occurred, and George Smith, the surgeon, said that the injury was consistent with Carpenter's version of events. Smith also said that Carpenter had suffered no other injuries, which was surprising if he had been involved in a life and death struggle with Constable Starkins.

The bloodstains on the accused man's clothes had all been explained. None of them could be shown to be Starkins' blood. Significantly, though all the witnesses agreed that there was a pool of blood at the site of the murder, there was none on Carpenter's boots. This point struck home, and the prosecutor interrupted the address to say that there was no evidence that the boots in question were those that Carpenter had worn that evening. The interjection was a mistake; Parry pointed out that the prosecution had introduced them as exactly that, and made a point of the presence of wheat and barley chaff on them. The prosecution could not have it both ways – if they were not the boots worn by Carpenter that evening, then the wheat and barley chaff on them was irrelevant. If they were, then the absence of blood was unexplained.

Quint's testimony was Parry's next target. It was most unlikely that Carpenter would confess his crime to a man that he did not know. Other witnesses had contradicted Quint's testimony. It could not be relied upon. Finally, Parry reminded the jury that their decision represented life or death to the accused.

Mr. Justice Williams summed up. He disapproved of Parry's final comment, which had no purpose other than to instil in the jury the fear of hanging an innocent man. They must ignore such considerations, and concentrate on whether the prosecution's case was proven. He reviewed the evidence for them, and sent them to consider their verdict. It took them half an hour.

The foreman, Mr. Ballard of Watford, told the court that "We all think that there is great ground of suspicion, but not direct evidence enough to warrant us in finding the prisoner guilty. We therefore return a verdict of not guilty." Carpenter was a free man. No one else was ever tried for the offence.

But was he guilty? The feeling at the time was that he probably did kill Constable Starkins. The press was hostile to him, but in view of their early reporting of the case, in which they assumed his guilt, perhaps we should not be surprised: they may well have felt the need to justify the early reports. His acquittal was attributed to excessive fairness, even favour, in the trial, and was used as an argument against capital punishment: it was claimed that it led to many guilty men going free because juries were unwilling to bear the responsibility for the defendant's life.

Carpenter was fortunate in having Sergeant Parry as his advocate. He had a firm grasp of the detail of the case, and was quick to seize any advantage that presented itself. His address to the jury was most persuasive.

All in all, the verdict was probably a fair one: there was good cause for suspicion, but not enough evidence to hang a man. So, to answer the question then: I agree with the jury - I think that Jeremiah Carpenter probably did kill Starkins, but there is sufficient doubt to justify his acquittal.

Chapter Eleven

"Joe, You Have Done It At Last..." Jane Castle of Ware, 1859

The marriage between Jane Whitcroft and Joseph Castle was not a happy one. It seems that the problems sprang from Joseph's obsessive (and unfounded) jealousy. He was reluctant to allow her out on her own, and was convinced of her infidelity. He was known as a sullen man, obstinate and wilful, and that can scarcely have made for marital bliss.

Joseph was born in Ware just after Christmas in 1834 of respectable parents, and attended school until the age of eleven. For three years he worked as a gardener's lad, and then enlisted in 33rd Regiment of the Foot. He served his country for more than four years, rising to the rank of corporal. On his return to civilian life he became a maltsman, but kept up his military connections by enlisting with the militia. His work in the brewing industry took him to Luton, where he met Jane Whitcroft.

Jane lived with her sister, and was a little younger than Joseph, being only nineteen when they met. She must have been smitten with him, however, because she left Luton and went to live in Ware, where in 1857 they married. They set up home with Castle's mother.

The relationship was tempestuous, with frequent and loud arguments. Before long Mrs. Castle decided she could abide the upheaval no longer, and asked them to leave.

The young couple took up lodgings at the Harrow, an inn in Kibes Lane. The arguments continued, if anything growing worse; the landlady of the Harrow even went so far as to suggest to Jane that she should return to her parents in Luton for fear of her life. Joseph frequently threatened to do away with Jane, and slept with knives beneath his pillow. The young girl must have been terrified.

Once more the quarrels forced them to move, this time to the home of Castle's uncle and aunt, James and Frances Castle. By early August 1859 Jane decided she could bear no more. Echoing the words of the landlady of the Harrow, Frances Castle too had told her that she might be wise to go home to Luton. Joseph himself said it might be best if she left, as he "had strange feels in his head, and feared he might do her some harm." When she tried to leave however he shredded her clothes to keep her in the house.

Eventually she decided once more to leave, and this time she took no chances. She planned her departure over the period of about a week. On 8 August, at 11:30 a.m., whilst Joseph was out looking for work, she left him to go back to her parents. Mary Ann Castle, Joseph's cousin, went with her as far as Hertford, because, Jane said, she was afraid of what might happen if her husband followed and caught up with her. As they travelled Jane kept a nervous eye on the road behind her.

By 3 p.m. Jane reached Cromer Hyde, about thirteen miles from Ware. She stayed there for almost two hours in the company of Esther Archer, the local schoolmistress. The Whitcroft family had lived in the area for some fifteen years, but had left when Jane was still quite young; presumably Esther Archer was an old family friend. Shortly before 5 p.m. Jane got a lift on the back of a coal waggon that was going in her direction.

Joseph was not far behind. Coming in from looking for work at about 2 p.m., his first thought was to check on his wife. When he found that she was not in the house, he questioned his aunt. Frances eventually admitted that Jane had left him and gone to Luton. Initially Joseph's reaction was one of acceptance, but it did not last, and he soon set off after her. By 7 p.m. he had reached Cromer Hyde, where he interrogated Esther Archer, being convinced that one of the silhouettes of young women he could see through her window was his wife. In the end Esther had to ask all the women in her household to show themselves in order to satisfy his suspicions. He seemed restless, and uneasy, and Esther slept badly that night for fear he might return.

Jane reached her parents' home at about 9 p.m. in a distressed state and in tears. After a brief reunion the family retired early; it is unlikely that they would have slept very well had they known that Joseph had arrived in Luton, and by 10 p.m. was in his father-in-law's strawplait dying house where he intended to spend the night. In the event he took several strolls around the town, and by seven the next morning was back at the house, exhausted after a sleepless night, having walked more than thirty-four miles in twenty four hours, and with nothing to eat.

Jane's parents left the house early. Jane was in bed, and her sister Emily was in the kitchen. Joseph came in and asked where his wife was, and Emily told him. Where was Mr. Whitcroft, he next wanted to know? He had gone to London on business. Castle seemed pale and agitated, but spoke politely and gently to Emily. After some desultory conversation, Joseph asked to see Jane. Emily agreed to tell her that he was there, and did so. Jane made no appearance, so after a while, Joseph took off his boots and went upstairs. He asked Jane if he might get into bed with her, as he was exhausted. She said no, but he got in anyway.

Exactly what passed between them over the next few minutes we do not know for sure, as they spoke only in very low tones. We do know that Joseph asked Jane to return home with him. She said that she was too foot-sore, but agreed to go part of the way back to Ware with her husband on the understanding that he carried on alone when she left him. They set off at 9:45 a.m. Jane wore a dress, bonnet and high shawl.

The couple walked under the railway bridge near the Windmill public house, and took the path towards Summeries (now Someries) Farm, where Sarah Juggins saw them pass. Jane was not seen alive again. A short time later, she was found in a chalk dell beside the road. She lay on her back with her throat cut, with her legs tucked beneath her. John Purser's cart was used to carry her body to the Heron Beer House in Luton. Meanwhile, Police Superintendent Pope and a surveyor, John Cumberland, examined the scene, took measurements and prepared a plan of the surrounding area.

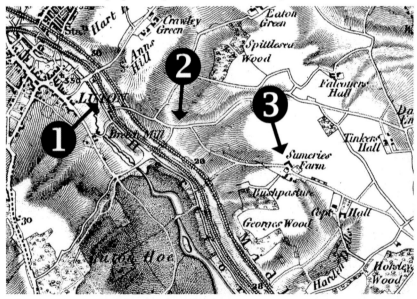

Above: The area to the southeast of Luton. 1- Windmill Road, now the A505; 2 – the path Joseph and Jane Castle took on their last walk together; 3 – Sumeries, now Sommeries, Farm. The murder took place just over the border in Bedfordshire. (courtesy Ordnance Survey).

On the road there were signs of a struggle, and a quantity of fresh blood. A trail of blood led to the dell where Jane lay, just twenty-seven yards away. Pope was struck by "the immense amount of blood" around her. More blood was found further along the path. In the belief that the killer had fled in that direction, Pope followed the path some twelve miles to Welwyn.

Pope was right – Castle had indeed taken the path to Welwyn. When he arrived, he went into the White Hart, where he had a pint of beer. He was known there, and attracted no great attention other than seeming quiet and reserved. His clothing was dirty and wet, as though he had been in a river.

Back in the street he accosted two women, asking for the location of the police stationhouse. They noticed that his hand was bleeding badly, and they directed him to the home of Police Constable Bennett. After another stop, this time at the Black Horse, Castle went to the constable's house.

Bennett recognized Castle, and invited him in for something to eat and drink. Castle turned down the offer of sustenance. He hinted that he had done worse than quarrel with his wife, but was not specific. He was anxious to avoid the Luton Police. Bennett noticed too that Castle's clothes were wet and bloodstained, and he seemed agitated. After a while he asked for pen and paper, and wrote a message to his brother:

> ~~Ware~~ Welwyng, August 9th, 1859
> Dear Brother, - I write these few lines to you hoping this will find you in good health as this leaves me very sadley Placed at this present moment. I wish you would be kind enough to take a ride to Luton in your Cart with all Possible speed – do not delay one moment.
> I Remain your unhappy Brother,
> J. CASTLE
> Welwyng.

The letter was originally addressed from Ware, but Castle crossed that out and substituted "Welwyng." Bennett had seen and heard enough: he locked Castle up in the local cage.

At about 2:30 p.m. Superintendent Pope arrived, and took Castle into custody on a charge of murder. On the way back to Luton, he said "I was never in one hour's trouble before in my life; and that would not have happened if she had kept away from Luton."

Meanwhile, at the crime scene, a group of men who had come to view the gory sight found a knife behind a hedge some yards from where Jane had been found. It was a kitchen knife, about a foot long, and it was bloodstained. They passed it to Constable George James. It proved to be an important piece of evidence.

Joseph Castle appeared before Bedford Lent Assizes in March 1860. Sergeant at Law Tozer and Dr. Abdy appeared for the prosecution, and Mr. Mills for the defence.

Witnesses appeared to testify that the marriage was a stormy one; that Jane Castle had left on the previous 9 August; and that Joseph had followed her. Others told of his arrival at the Whitcroft household the following morning, and how Jane had left with him. They were seen on the path to the Summeries. Pope and Bennett recounted their involvement.

Mr. Patrick Benson, a Luton surgeon, gave medical evidence. He had examined the body at the scene and found "a wound extending from under the left ear to the wind pipe on that side…" This wound was rough, as though caused by a sawing action. On further examination with his finger he found a second puncture wound near the windpipe that extended inwards as far as the spine, severing the artery and causing death. After the body had been removed to the Heron Inn and washed, a further examination revealed a number of cuts to the hands. He gave his view that Jane had been forced to her knees, and then pulled backwards and her throat first cut, then stabbed. He thought that the body could not have been forced into that position in any other way. In fact he was wrong. Nor did his explanation account for the bloodstains in the roadway. He withdrew an opinion he had expressed at the Magistrates' Court that Jane could have killed herself. He now firmly believed that to be impossible.

Finally, James Castle, the accused's uncle, appeared to identify the knife. He had, he said, given it to his nephew. He knew it by the repair he had made to the handle.

Such was the case for the prosecution. Joseph Castle had the opportunity and the motive (albeit unwarranted) to kill his wife. His clothes were bloodstained. He had made some damning remarks to Constable Bennett. The knife used in the murder had been in his possession shortly before the crime.

Mr. Mills' defence was that it was more probable that Jane had killed herself than it was that Joseph had killed her. There were, after all, no witnesses. He drew attention to the surgeon's withdrawn opinion that she could have cut her own throat. It may even have been Jane who had brought the knife from Ware. The cuts to Castle's fingers were, he suggested, caused by an altercation over the knife, after which he left her alone and went on his way. Witnesses had testified that she was distressed, and it might have been this distress that caused her to take her own life. It was clear that Castle was passionately fond of his wife to the extent of obsession, and this very obsession was, perhaps, enough to drive her to end what had become a miserable existence. He pointed out that suicide is more common than murder.

The Judge summed up. The jury must ignore the consequence of their verdict: that was for the law of the land to worry about. Their task was to decide whether Joseph Castle murdered his wife beyond reasonable doubt. Neither anger nor jealousy was an excuse to kill. If the wounds to Joseph's hands were the result of him defending himself, the verdict should be manslaughter. For a man to be irresponsible for his acts by reason of insanity, he must be unaware that what he was doing is wrong. The burden of proof in that case was upon the defence.

After a detailed summary of the evidence, the jury retired. It took them just ten minutes to find Joseph Castle guilty of murder. He was sentenced to be hanged.

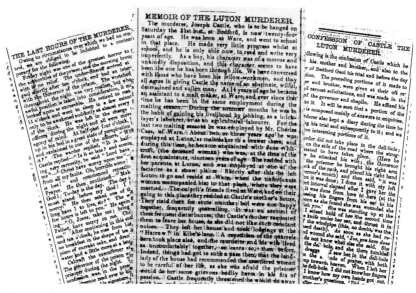

Above: the newspapers gave extensive coverage to the Castle murder. These cuttings are from the Hertford Mercury.

For some time Castle did not seem to appreciate the fate that awaited him. He was cheerful, and slept and ate well. But on 22 March Mr Roberts, the governor of Bedford Prison, had the unenviable task of telling him that the date and time of his execution had been set at 31 March, at twelve noon. Castle replied, "Oh! I have another week to live, thank God! I'll give myself up to God. I deserve it." He became difficult, even truculent at times. He sulked, and refused meals. The governor, chaplain and prison staff did all they could to ensure that his last days on earth passed as pleasantly as possible.

Castle's mother and brother visited him, and in the presence of the governor and chaplain they questioned him about the events leading to Jane's death. The story he told was a chilling one.

The assault had been carried out in the roadway. Castle had put his right arm around Jane's neck and mouth, and cut her throat with the knife in his left hand. As soon as she found she was wounded, Castle continued, "she said, 'I'll punish you.' She was standing up at the time I did it; I seized hold of her the second time and entered the knife under her ear... As soon as she received the second wound she said, 'Joe, you have done it at last!' I do not know what else she said. She walked towards the dell-hole, and there she tumbled in. She was not dragged. I saw her in the dell-hole on her knees in the attitude of prayer, with both hands lifted up to heaven."

Above: Joseph Castle kills his wife. The quality of illustrations in contemporary broadsheets was not always high, nor were they necessarily accurate. According to Castle, he held the knife in his left hand when he stabbed Jane. The wounds were to the left side of her neck.

He did not know how his fingers came to be cut, nor those of Jane. His mother pressed him to tell her whether he had brought the knife from Ware. He eventually admitted that he had. After his visitors had left, Castle seemed in the mood to talk. He revealed to the governor and chaplain more of the missing details of the events of 9 August the previous year. Jane had urged him to leave Luton, promising that if he did so she would walk part of the way with him. He replied that he would rather die than leave her. Jane pressed him to leave the town, and he had eventually agreed to do so. They had started out at about 10 a.m. As they walked, Castle tried to persuade her to come back to him, but she was adamant: she was sick of the life they led, and she was afraid of him. She upbraided him for following her. He tried to kiss her, and as they walked he put his arm around her waist. As they came to the dell, he asked her again to return to Ware with him, to which she replied, "You do not want me."

"I made no more propositions to her, and cared no more for life, as life seemed a burden to me. I laid hold of her… and kissed her then. The deed followed."

Over the last days Joseph Castle kept a diary, an exercise in self-justification.

"I dare say, if she had went away openly I should not have followed her; she might have saved me from this with a little discression on her part. But I suppose she was young and giddy. I am very sorry she was so thoughtless, but I am here, and God knows the consiquences." Not a word does he say about the irrational jealousy that drove Jane to leave him. Nor does he mention destroying her clothes the first time she tried to leave, nor the knives he kept beneath the pillow, nor the constant quarrels.

William Calcraft, the executioner, arrived at the prison on Friday, 30 March in order to make the necessary preparations.

Above: Bedford Gaol, outside which Joseph Castle has hanged by William Calcraft. From a contemporary illustration.

Murder and Misdemeanour in Hertfordshire

The day of the execution was wet, but the trains into Bedford were packed. People from the nearby villages walked or rode into town. For those who were unable to attend, the newspapers covered the events in detail. The inns and alehouses did a roaring trade, and many of the sightseers were more than a little merry by midday. Broadsheets describing the murder, the trial and impending execution sold for a penny apiece. Some were in verse:

> Sure Satan must have tempted me,
> Upon that fateful day.
> Jane Castle for to murder,
> And take life away.
> All with a deadly weapon,
> It was my full intent,
> And gave her not the shortest
> On earth for to repent.
> I'm sentenced for to die
> Upon the gallows high.
>
> I was confined in Bedford Gaol
> My trial to await,
> For the awful crime of murder
> My sufferings were great,
> The Jury found me Guilty,
> And I am doom'd to die
> An awful death of public gaze,
> Upon the gallows high.
> Before it is too late,
> Think on my untimely fate.

Shrimps, pies, nuts, cakes and fruit were on sale to the throng, and a carnival atmosphere prevailed. The windows of the houses opposite the gallows were packed. On the roofs exponents of the new art of photography set up their apparatus, ready to catch the fatal moment. Barriers were placed in front of the gaol to control the crowd.

A table was carried out and placed behind the barriers, and from this temporary stage the Reverend Fitzpatrick delivered a sermon to the crowd.

As noon approached, the execution procession emerged from the gaol into the view of the 15,000 spectators. First came the attendants of the Sheriff, carrying javelins; next the warders; and then Castle was led from the gaol and onto the scaffold, his arms pinioned to his sides. Finally, Calcraft mounted the gallows. He slipped the rope around Castle's neck, and in a moment his life was over. The body was left hanging for an hour before being taken into the prison for certification and burial.

That evening, the friends and family of Jane Castle held a celebratory ball. As they left, each and every guest was presented with a commemorative bobbin.

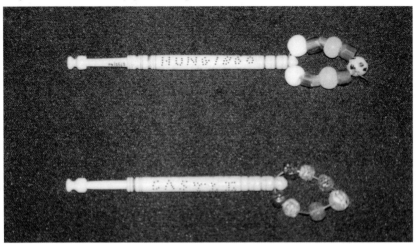

Above: Two examples of the lace makers' bobbins commemorating the execution of Joseph Castle. The design of the bobbins differs slightly, but the lettering seems to be by the same hand. It reads "JOSEPH CASTLE HUNG 1860." (author, courtesy of Luton Museum)

Chapter Twelve

Murder or Manslaughter? Constable Snow, Bennington, 1871

In the late nineteenth century the village of Bennington was a small community some four miles to the east of Stevenage, itself at that time, though growing slowly, little more than a village. Stevenage has now of course expanded beyond recognition, but Bennington is much the same as it was then. The area was predominantly rural, with a high proportion of working men being employed on the land. Such crime as there was tended towards drunkenness, theft and poaching, the latter being viewed as a serious offence at that time.

It was to this area that Police Constable Benjamin Snow came in 1868, with his wife and three children. He was a hard-working officer, and was well liked by those who met him in a non-professional capacity.

The other central character in the tragedy that was to unfold was James Chapman. He knew the Bennington area well, being a native of Luffenhall, about four miles to the north, though he now lived at no. 1, Goff's Cottages, Nightingale Road, Wood Green, on the northern outskirts of London. Like P.C. Snow, he was a family man, with a wife and five children. He was in the habit of leaving them for weeks at a time, while he travelled the southern counties in search of game. He was well known to the police, and a warrant for his arrest on a charge of game trespass, issued by the Ware Petty Sessional Division in November 1865, was still outstanding. Chapman was thirty-seven years old, and was described as a rugged, foul-mouthed man.

The morning of Tuesday, 10 January 1871, was cold, and snow lay on the ground. As he prepared to go on duty, Benjamin Snow told his wife that Chapman was in the area. Inspector Reynolds had instructed him, with Police Constables Williams and Worby, to watch out for him. The plan was to visit local farms and search the outbuildings for the fugitive.

The officers were right: Chapman was in the area. He met with William Warner at about 10:00 a.m., who asked him, "How are you getting on?" "Damned bad," was the reply.

Just after 12 noon, Robert Blaxill, a roadman, saw Constable Snow on the Whempstead Road. He was sure of the hour, because he had asked Snow what time it was.

Right: the Bennington area. 1 – the Old Bell Inn; 2 – Snow's police house; 3 – the Whempstead Road; 4 – Whempstead. Stevenage lies to the west. (courtesy Ordnance

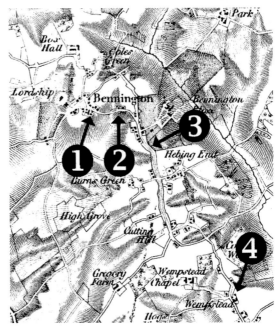

James Gilbey, aged 16, a farm labourer, was in the lane between Whempstead and Bennington at about 12 o'clock, when he saw James Chapman coming across the fields. Chapman asked Gilbey who the local gamekeeper was, to which the lad replied "Master Palmer." Gilbey noticed that Chapman was carrying a gun, the barrels in one pocket and the stock in the other. The two walked together down the lane towards Bennington, turning up Back Lane. Chapman asked the boy to wait for him there, as he was going to "meet a man," and wanted Gilbey to show him the way to Green End when he returned. Shortly afterwards he heard a shot. He followed Chapman, and met him coming back down the lane; he had blood on his fingers. Gilbey showed him the way to Green End, than left him, saying, "there is Mr. Snow, the policeman, coming." "Oh, is there," Chapman replied.

As the boy hurried back up the lane, he passed Constable Snow. He turned, and from a distance of about ten yards he saw Snow get hold of Chapman's jacket. Gilbey ran for home, fearing that Chapman had been poaching, and that Snow would arrest him as an accomplice.

Snow had seen Chapman and Gilbey together, and asked William Beadle, who was working in his garden, if he knew them. He did not. Snow went after them. A few minutes later Gilbey came walking back up the lane, alone. He was followed twenty minutes later by Snow, who was holding a handkerchief to the side of his head. He said, "Beadle, I'm shot." "That's a bad job," replied Beadle. Snow walked on towards the village.

At about 12:45 p.m. Snow passed Robert Blaxill. He spoke to him in a confused manner two or three times, but he could not make himself understood. There was a small quantity of blood near Snow's left ear, and Blaxill asked him if he had "the earache." Eventually Snow managed to say, "I have got shot," and walked on towards his house, which he reached at about 1 p.m. Blaxill said later that he had heard no shots fired.

As soon as he got into the house his wife, Mary, noticed there was something wrong. He looked ill, and held his head on one side. She asked him what was the matter, and he replied, "I don't know, dear." He went upstairs, and Mary sent for the doctor, Henry Hodges.

Dr. Hodges examined Snow, and found a large bruise on the left side of his head. There was a lot of blood gathered beneath the skin, though the wound itself was small. In response to Hodges' questions, Snow tried to tell him what had happened, but he seemed unable to form the words. To each question he replied little more than "Yes, sir," and mumbled about a warrant. The doctor stayed with him for about an hour. When he called back that evening, the constable was dead.

Right: Inspector Reynolds, who played a major part in the investigation. At one point Reynolds, his son and his grandson were all serving with Hertfordshire Constabulary at the same time.

On learning that one of his officers had been killed, Inspector Reynolds visited the scene the following morning. He found the marks of a struggle in the snow. He followed the tracks of a man wearing old and mended boots, with an unusual pattern of nails, and noted that the wearer walked in a splay-footed manner similar to that of Chapman. Further investigations were made impossible by a further fall of snow.

Reynolds advised the Metropolitan Police that one of his officers had been murdered, and that Chapman was the chief suspect. By Friday 13 January Chapman was in custody. He was arrested by Sergeant Turner at Goff's Cottages in Wood Green. During a search of the house a gun, in two pieces, was seized, along with flasks for powder and shot. Inspector Reynolds took possession of the gun, the flasks and Chapman's boots, and Chapman was taken to Stevenage to be charged with murder.

An inquest opened at the Bell public house on the same day that Chapman was arrested. The jury were taken to the police house to view the body. The first witness, Dr. Hodges, told the coroner that a post mortem was yet to be performed, so the court adjourned until Monday 16 January at Bennington School house. Chapman was present for identification purposes, but was removed before witnesses gave evidence.

Above: the Bell at Bennington. The initial inquest on Constable Snow was held here on 13 January 1871. (author)

Dr. Hodges told the jury of his visits to Snow, and of the results of the post mortem he had carried out with the assistance of John Woodhouse, M.D.

There were two centres of bruising about 1½ inches apart, leading to the impression that two blows had been struck. The skull was fractured, and beneath it was a mass of coagulated blood the size of a man's fist as a result of the rupture of some branches of the meningeal artery. It was this large clot that had led to Snow's bewildered state, and eventually to his death. The injuries were, thought Hodges, the result of blows rather than a fall, and a blunt instrument such as the butt of a gun might be responsible. Snow's claims that he had been shot were mistaken – perhaps he really thought that he had been shot, or possibly the concussion he had received left him in such confusion that he did not know what he was saying.

Constable George Williams testified that he held a warrant for the arrest of Chapman on a charge of poaching, and that Snow knew of its existence.

The next witnesses were Robert Blaxill, Inspector Reynolds, Sergeant Turner James Gilbey and William Warner, who told the court of their involvement in the affair. The court adjourned part way through Gilbey's evidence to allow the funeral to take place in Bennington churchyard.

When the inquest resumed, Chapman was given the opportunity to account for the evidence; he denied all knowledge of Snow's death.

The jury quickly returned a verdict of wilful murder against James Chapman, and two days later the magistrates committed him to appear before Hertford Assizes.

On the 2 March Chapman's trial began. It seemed at first that the result was a foregone conclusion. The accused was seen in the company of Snow, and had the motive of resisting arrest. Inspector Reynolds' testimony of the crime scene confirmed the witness accounts, and he said that he believed that the unusual footprints he had seen in the snow were made by Chapman's boots, which he had examined.

But the defence argued that Snow's attempt to detain Chapman had been illegal, because the warrant had not been in the constable's possession at the time of the arrest. Mr. Justice Hannen seemed inclined to agree, though he was not sure how the law stood. He pointed out that if the arrest was illegal, then Chapman had the right to resist. The defence referred to the case of *Galliard v. Laxton*, which laid down that though a warrant may be addressed to the constabulary as a whole, the arresting officer must have the document in his possession at the time when he apprehended the suspect. If he did not, the arrest was unlawful, and the suspect was entitled to resist "even unto death." The judge demurred at the suggestions of a right to kill. The prosecution countered by pointing out that the Prevention of Poaching Acts of 1862 and 1863 gave a constable statutory authority to make a search of a suspect, and, if appropriate, arrest him. The arguments on this point of law went back and forth for some time.

The jury deliberated only briefly. They were in no doubt that Chapman had killed Snow, probably by striking him on the head with the butt of his gun, but their verdict must have been influenced by Hannen's remark in his summing up that if the jury "believed that the injuries were inflicted in consequence of excitement and provocation, produced in the mind of the prisoner by the deceased man attempting to arrest him, being as he was, without a warrant, [they] would be justified in finding the prisoner guilty of manslaughter." And that was the verdict they reached.

It was only after the verdict had been announced that the judge said that "it would be a fearful thing indeed if men were to be allowed to suppose that because a police constable sought to arrest them without a warrant, that they were justified in using such violence as had been used in this case." He sentenced James Chapman to fifteen years' penal servitude.

Benjamin Snow lies buried in Bennington churchyard. His funeral was attended by Colonel Robertson, the Chief Constable, Superintendent Bygrave, Inspectors Reynolds, Hunt, Young and Oliver, and some forty of his colleagues, in addition to many villagers. His stone still stands to the southeast of the church, so badly eroded over 130 years that the inscription is scarcely legible. Unless you know where to look, you might miss it entirely. There is no longer any clue upon it as to how he met his untimely end.

Right: the grave of Benjamin Snow in Bennington churchyard. The inscription is badly eroded, but the constable's name is just legible. (author)

Murder and Misdemeanour in Hertfordshire

Mary Ann Snow, the constable's widow, later remarried; once more she chose a policeman, George Brooks.

Chapter Thirteen

Love Unrequited; Augusta Wiles and Edward Pindar, Hitchin, 1877

Augusta Wiles was a well-known woman in Hitchin. She was the daughter of Henry Wiles, the town's vicar, and sister-in-law to the Reverend Gainsford, the wealthy one-time curate of St. Mary's Church, and builder of St. Saviour's Church in Radcliffe Road. That part of the town was a growth area following the arrival of the railway in 1850, and Gainsford spent a good deal of time and money catering for the spiritual needs of its inhabitants.

Right: the victim, Miss Sarah Augusta Wiles. (North Hertfordshire Museum Service)

Murder and Misdemeanour in Hertfordshire

In 1877 Augusta (christened Sarah Augusta, but always known by her middle name) was in her mid forties, and lived in Walsworth Road, which ran from close to the town centre to the station. Edward Pindar was a 49-year-old Russian émigré who gave private language lessons to his clients, Miss Wiles amongst them. He had formed an attachment to his pupil some time before, and made his feelings known. He had proposed marriage, but been rejected. Future lessons had for a time been in doubt; unfortunately for Miss Wiles, the decision was taken to continue with them. It very nearly cost her her life.

On the Wednesday, 7 November, at about mid-day, Pindar came into the Police Station. At that time the station was in Silver Street, now Bancroft (the building had once been the bridewell, or house of correction, and was located at the north end of Skinner's Almshouses). Pindar's face was "smothered with blood", and he was bleeding freely from a serious cut in his hand. Pieces of hair were sticking to his fingers. He had, he said, come to give himself up after assaulting Miss Wiles.

The events leading up to the attack began on Monday, 5 November, when Pindar called on Miss Wiles and again proposed to her. She refused him once more. Two days later, at 11.30 a.m., Pindar came to the house as usual to give Miss Wiles her language lesson.

Within a few minutes he turned to her and said, "There must be an end of this; you must marry me." She declined, and Pindar seized her, and tried to kiss her. When she resisted, he drew a knife from his pocket. The assault that followed is best told in Miss Wiles' own words:

> "He tried to stab me in the head, and I tried to escape and fell down upon the floor. While [I was] on the floor he stabbed me several times upon the head. I got the knife from him; whether I got it by force or whether he let me take it I don't know. I had used my hands to protect my head. In doing this my hands were injured. After I got the knife away he attacked my eyes with his fists. He twisted his fists round in my eyes as if he wished to put my eyes out... Then he left off and stood a little distance away, and shook a tuft of hair in front of me. After that he walked out of the room."

During the assault the knife, which folded, partially closed on Pindar's fingers when the blade was stopped by her skull. This caused the injury to his hand noticed by some of the witnesses.

The maid, Selina King, was too frightened to intervene in any way. She heard screams, and saw her mistress covered in blood. The knife, which she later gave to Inspector George Young, had been placed on a table in the hall by Miss Wiles.

Miss Wiles' injuries were serious. Mr Shillitoe, the surgeon, was called. He found she was bleeding from several wounds. One was on the left side of her forehead, another above her forehead on the right. Three more were in the back of the head, penetrating to the bone. One of the wounds on her hand had come close to severing the palmar artery. Both her eyes were blackened, and she could not open them.

Inspector Young had meanwhile secured Pindar at the Police Station and, leaving him in the custody of a constable, he followed a trail of blood to Miss Wiles' home. There he was given the bloodstained knife by the maid. The furniture in the drawing room was in disarray, and in a pool of blood on the floor he found a tuft of hair.

Some initial newspaper reports were surprisingly sympathetic to Edward Pindar, and contained inaccuracies concerning Miss Wiles' wounds. Prosecution was thought to be unlikely, they said, and Miss Wiles' injuries were reported to be slight. Pindar was a clever linguist, and had during his residence in Hitchin "obtained appointments in some of the best families in town." He had, however, "the appearance of a man of morose disposition," and gave "the impression that he was somewhat mad." The cause of the attack was a mystery to the press. Miss Wiles was variously reported to have been learning French or German.

Pindar was remanded in custody. About three weeks before his trial at the Central Criminal Court he attempted, unsuccessfully, to take his own life.

There were two charges against him: wounding Miss Wiles with intent to murder; and wounding with intent to do her grievous bodily harm. He chose to represent himself, and pleaded not guilty.

The prosecution outlined the case against Pindar, including his motive. He had told Inspector Young during a conversation in a police cell that he had intended to disfigure the woman, not to kill her. Before the magistrates he claimed that he had acted "in a moment of intense and justifiable exasperation." Whether he believed that the assault would change her mind, or whether he had intended to make sure that if he could not have her, then no-one else would want her, he did not say.

Witnesses for the prosecution took the stand: Miss Wiles herself, and Selina King, the maid; Inspector Young and Mr. Shillitoe. They testified to the events already recounted.

Pindar was asked if there were any witnesses he wanted to call in his defence. He passed a list to the usher, but no-one answered the call outside the court. Pindar claimed that the witnesses were important to his defence, and the names were called again, once more without response. The court was impatient:

> The Judge: We cannot wait for them.
> Pindar: I have been completely shut out from legal assistance of any kind and those witnesses would be most important for my defence.

Once more the usher called for the witnesses.

> The Judge: No-one answers, you see. We cannot wait for them. Do you wish to say anything to the jury?
> Pindar: Yes. I wish to say that I had no intention of taking the life of Miss Wiles or to do her grievous bodily harm. I had had many troubles, and this occurred in a fit of frenzy... I have been shut out from legal advice and do not find myself in a state of either body or mind to go on with the defence.

What the nature of the defence witnesses' testimony would have been is not recorded, but it is probable that they were character witnesses, perhaps selected from amongst his clients. Pindar had not attempted to deny that he had stabbed Miss Wiles, so his defence options were limited.

The judge summed up for the jury. There was no doubt that the prisoner had inflicted the wounds described upon Miss Wiles. The only question they must decide was whether the defendant had intended to kill, or to injure her. They did not take long to reach their verdict: guilty of wounding with intent to do grievous bodily harm.

The Clerk of Arraigns asked Pindar if he had anything to say before sentence was passed, to which he replied that he had "suffered a great deal in Hitchin and elsewhere, and that my mind has become impaired. Really I am on many occasions not accountable for my actions. Looking at the matter from a medical point of view I do not know what can be done, but I must take whatever penalty the Court may inflict upon me. I hope, however, the Court will be as lenient as possible. I have suffered intensely in Hitchin, intensely."

The judge sent for Miss Wiles, who had left the Court, as he felt it right that she should be asked if she had anything to say before he passed sentence. Before she arrived however counsel for the prosecution reported that he had already received instructions from her on that subject. She wished, he said, to leave the matter entirely in the hands of the Court. The Judge passed sentence:

Love Unrequited; Augusta Wiles and Edward Pindar

Edward Pindar, you have been found guilty of wounding with intent to cause grievous bodily harm; the jury have taken a lenient and merciful view of your case... No-one who has heard this case can doubt that you are guilty of the offence of which you have been convicted... I must still pass a severe sentence. The sentence of this Court is that you be kept in penal servitude for five years.

There can be no doubt that George Pindar stabbed Augusta Wiles. It seems likely too that he was telling the truth when he told Inspector Young that his intention was to disfigure, not to kill.

It is worthy of mention however that the interview during which Pindar's intent was discussed took place in a police cell, with no other witnesses. That Young almost certainly reported the conversation accurately does not change the fact that accepting such an interview as evidence was in those days, as now, fraught with risk.

Was Pindar insane? Perhaps he was. He certainly lost control in his passion for Augusta Wiles, and her refusal to respond to it. But passion and fury cannot be a defence, or every angry man would be innocent.

Did the failure of Pindar's witnesses to appear prejudice his trial? It is unlikely that they would have materially affected the sentence. Nothing would have saved him from penal servitude, and the minimum sentence under the Act of 1864 was five years; it was not to be reduced to three years until 1891. Once the judge had decided penal servitude was appropriate, five years was the lowest sentence he could give.

Pindar presumably served his sentence. He may have been released early if he behaved himself. There is no reason to believe he troubled Miss Wiles again.

Augusta Wiles never did marry. She lived until 1909, when at the age of 77 she was knocked down by a cyclist in London. Her skull was fractured, and she died after laying unconscious for two or three weeks. Her obituary recalled her as a great traveller; increasing age did not restrict her in this activity, nor in her work for her true passion in life - the church.

Chapter Fourteen

The Murder of Edward Anstee, Marshall's Wick, St Albans, 1880

Edward Anstee was a sprightly gentleman of some 68 years of age, though he looked older. He lived at Marshall's Wick Farm, a few miles outside St. Albans on the Sandridge Road. At the time of his death he was a dairy farmer, but in his younger days he had been first a blacksmith, then a gentleman's valet, and finally a butcher. He was well read and intelligent; a kindly man, with a wide circle of friends. His farm supplied milk to both St. Albans and London. He was married, but with no children. In the early hours of the morning on 22 August 1880, he was shot dead in his home.

Thomas Wheeler was in his mid forties, and although he now lived in Lewisham with his wife and children, he was familiar with south Hertfordshire. His brother lived nearby, and he had worked in various menial capacities on local farms for many years. He was, however, something of a wanderer, and by 1880 he had taken to supporting himself and his family by theft and burglary.

But to understand the chain of events that led to Anstee's murder, and to the arrest of Thomas Wheeler for the crime, we must go back to 8 June of that year. The blacksmith's shop of William Page in St. Peters Street, St. Albans, was broken into, and two hammers were stolen. Later the same night the home of Jacob Reynolds was burgled. Reynolds lived at Bernard's Heath in St. Albans, and amongst the items stolen were a Snider rook rifle, a plated cruet and a dish.

Reynolds had gone to bed that night at about 11 p.m., but was awakened an hour later when the appropriately named Miss M. A. Yell, the governess, raised the alarm. She had heard intruders downstairs, and on opening her window had seen a man crossing the croquet lawn. On investigation, Reynolds found that a hurdle had been placed against the window to gain entry, and the schoolroom ransacked. He secured the house and went back to bed. In the morning he made an inventory of the stolen items and informed the police. In the flower bed Miss Yell found a hammer that did not belong to the household: she gave it to Reynolds, who passed it on to Police Constable Weeds. Page later identified it as one of the two stolen from his workshop.

In the middle of August another blacksmith suffered the theft of a hammer. John Smith, of Wheathampstead, last recalled seeing the tool on the 16th of the month, but it may have been stolen a day or two later. In any event, it turned up after a burglary at Samwell Farm on 18 August.

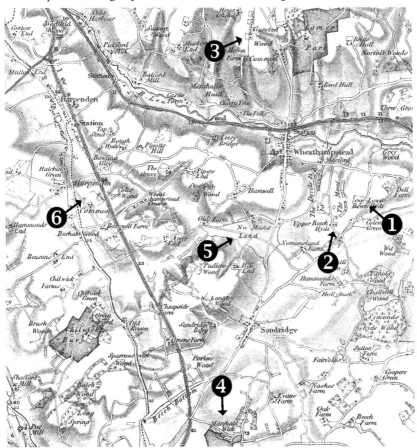

Above: the area where the events took place. 1 –Samwell Farm (marked Lower Beech Hyde Farm on this map); 2 – Beech Hyde Farm; 3 – Gustard's, or Gursted's Wood. 4 – Marshall's Wick; 5 & 6 – No Man's Land and Harpenden Common, where Wheeler claimed to have spent the nights of 20 & 21 August respectively. St. Albans lies to the south of Marshall's Wick. (courtesy Ordnance Survey).

Samwell Farm (sometimes called Samuel Farm or Lower Beech Hyde Farm) is to the southeast of Wheathampstead, and at that time was occupied by Edward Woollatt and his family. His father, Mr. George Woollatt, occupied Beech Hyde Farm about ten minutes walk away. Mr. Woollatt junior and his family had already gone to bed when at about midnight they were roused by an unknown man, who told them that the ricks at his father's farm were on fire. From his window Edward could see the flames, and he immediately went to see if he could help, leaving the back door unlocked behind him. On his way to Beech Hyde he met his father coming the other way, carrying a cash box that he was bringing to his son's house for safekeeping.

Meanwhile an intruder had entered Samwell farmhouse. Susan Woollatt heard him moving about, and, thinking that it was her husband, she called out, "Ted, is that you?" A strange voice answered her, so she quickly locked her bedroom door. She heard the prowler opening the doors to the downstairs rooms. He then came up the stairs and tried the door to her room. She asked what he wanted. "I want a barrel of beer, a bottle of wine or ten shillings," was the reply. She asked him his name, and understood him to say "Friz." Terrified, Mrs. Woollatt fled the room using the back stairs and hid in the garden.

The unknown man next went to the room of Harriet Lines, a servant of the Woollatt family. She saw a short man, wearing a dark coat and a hat. He had a red and white handkerchief tied around his face, hiding it as high as his nose. He held a lamp in one hand and a hammer in the other. With great courage she got out of bed and shut and locked the door in his face. The man went downstairs.

When Harriet thought he had left the house, she went to Susan Woollatt's door; finding it locked, she returned to her room in time to see from her window George Woollatt arriving from Beech Hyde. She went downstairs to meet him, and told him what had happened.

Mr. Woollatt senior had meanwhile entered the house via the back door, and seen a man holding a light in the passage. As soon as George had spoken the light was extinguished. George had asked him to light it again, and the man had requested a match. When George had said he had none, the man calmly walked past him and left the building. George called out for his daughter-in-law, Susan Woollatt, but it was not until he used her Christian name that she emerged from her hiding place in the garden.

When Edward returned, he found that his double-barrelled shotgun had been stolen, along with an 8-pound joint of pickled pork. Though he did not realise it at the time, a reticule basket had also been taken. The following morning they found the hammer that had been stolen from John Smith.

It seemed that the intruder had deliberately fired the ricks at Beech Hyde with the intention of drawing out the occupants of Samwell Farm, leaving it vulnerable to his predations. Considerable damage was done at Beech Hyde; several hayricks, a barn and some outbuildings were destroyed.

The next page in the saga is the murder of Edward Anstee at Mashall's Wick Farm. In 1880 the buildings were quite modern, not overlarge, consisting of some seven or eight rooms. There were two storeys and an attic level. The normal household consisted of Mr. Anstee, his wife Mary, and a young servant girl, Elizabeth Coleman, usually known as Eliza. At the time of the murder Mary was visiting friends near Reading. Her sister, Mrs. Susan Lindsay, was staying with Mr. Anstee, and acting as housekeeper.

On the evening of 21 August the household retired early. Eliza went to bed first, sometime between 9 and 10 p.m., after having secured the windows and door at the back of the house. Ten minutes later Edward Anstee locked up at the front, and he and Mrs. Lindsay followed the serving girl upstairs. They had no idea of the terrifying ordeal that lay ahead of them.

At about 3 a.m. Mr. Anstee was awakened by a voice calling to him from the yard, "Master, wake up; one of the cows is ill." Anstee opened the window and looked out. "What's amiss? What's amiss?" he asked. From the darkness came the blast of a shotgun, striking the elderly man in the face. He fell back into the room and slumped against the wall, dead. Such was the violence of the discharge that Anstee was killed instantly, the left side of his face and his brain shattered.

The shot woke both Susan Lindsay and Eliza. Mrs. Lindsay stayed in her bed; Eliza got up and looked from her window into the yard, but could see nothing. Still concerned, she bolted the door of her attic room and lay in bed listening. Both women noted that the farm dog had not barked, which surprised them. The next morning they were to find it listless and drowsy, as though drugged.

Shortly after the shot, a man climbed into Mr. Anstee's bedroom window. He went downstairs and collected the lamp from the dining room, then returned to the unoccupied bedroom next to Mr. Anstee's room; after a quick look round, he opened Mrs. Lindsay's door. He said, "Mr. Anstee's gone to the cow." She could not see him very clearly, but she thought he was a small man, dressed in dark clothes.

The intruder next checked the bathroom, and then went back downstairs. He was there some time, making a good deal of noise as he searched the ground floor rooms for items of value.

When he returned, he had left the lamp behind. He evidently thought that Mrs. Lindsay was Mary Anstee, because he addressed her by name, saying he wanted to lie down. He pulled at the bedclothes. She called for Mr. Anstee several times before the intruder told her that he was "out." She then called out "Eliza! Eliza!" He left the room, and Mrs. Lindsay hurried to the door and locked it.

After a while the man returned, and seemed surprised to find her door secured. "Oh, you've fastened the door," he said. "How came you to do that?" She made no reply, and he went back downstairs. He was there for some minutes, making more noise as he ransacked the building.

A fourth time he came back upstairs, this time asking where Anstee kept his cash box. Mrs. Lindsay did not know, and said so. In that case, he said, she must give him money, or he would "burst open your door and give you a knock on the head." He struck the door several times with a hammer, and said he wanted five shillings; she pushed a two-shilling coin between the door and its jamb.

Yet again the man went downstairs, and yet again he returned. This time he wanted beer, and Mrs. Lindsay directed him to the cellar where the ale was kept. Some minutes later, she saw the man crossing the lawn with a bundle under each arm. Ten minutes after that he returned for two more bundles.

Mrs. Lindsay checked her watch, and found the time to be about half past three. She remained in her room until four, then opened her door and called Eliza.

The serving girl had prudently stayed in her room the whole time. She was under the impression that there had been two shots, but otherwise her recollections were very close to those of the housekeeper. She had heard the intruder come up the stairs several times, and the exchanges between him and Mrs. Lindsay. She heard the front door bang several times as he left with his plunder.

When Mrs. Lindsay called, she came down in her nightdress. After exchanging a few words, Eliza returned to her room to dress. As she did so, she heard George Bailey, the cowman, arrive for work. Opening her window, she waved, and called out for him to come into the house. As she finished dressing, Bailey went to the front of the house, and, finding the door open, he went in, calling for Mr. Anstee.

Mrs. Lindsay had meanwhile looked into Edward Anstee's room and seen his body lying before the window, covered by his bedclothes. She did not investigate further, but went downstairs to talk to George Bailey. She told him that Mr. Anstee was upstairs, so he went up to his master's room to check. As he did so, Eliza passed him on her way down.

Bailey found the room much disturbed, the drawers pulled out and their contents scattered around the room. He saw the body by the window, but when he pulled back the covering he found he could not tell who it was. His first thought was that it was the body of the intruder, so he went back downstairs. Only when Mrs. Lindsay told him that it was Mr. Anstee did he return and look more closely. He was finally able to recognise the dead man by a scar on his chin. Bailey checked the other bedrooms to see if anyone else was in the house. He found that they too had been ransacked.

The cowman went out into the yard, where he spoke to the farm boy. He set him on a pony and sent him to St. Albans to fetch Constable Pike and the doctor. After he had given the lad these instructions, he noticed that a ladder was propped against the front of the house, against Edward Anstee's window. He had last seen it the night before, when it had lain against a haystack about a hundred yards from the house. Now, he saw, seven or eight feet had been broken from one end to make it a more manageable size.

Meanwhile, in the passageway Eliza found a large hammer that she did not recognise. Lying by the open cellar door was a tin quart beer pot. She checked the first floor rooms, and she found that the plate cupboard had been opened and its contents were missing.

The farm lad arrived in St. Albans just before five, and summoned Mr. F. R. Webster, the surgeon, and the police. They immediately went to Marshall's Wick Farm, arriving at about five thirty. As the surgeon walked around the back of the house, he noticed blood on the window frame of Mr. Anstee's bedroom.

Webster went straight upstairs and examined the body. He was in no doubt that Anstee had died instantaneously. He concluded that the shot had been fired at close range, but not close enough to result in scorching of the flesh; he thought perhaps from about ten feet. There were pellet holes in the glass of the lower frame of the window, and blood and brains on the sill.

On the brickwork too there were bloodstains, and a pool of blood lay on the stones of the yard beneath the window. This must, he thought, have gushed from the dead man's head straight onto the ground below. That meant that Anstee must have leaned well out of the window just before he was shot. There were numerous pellets embedded in the ceiling of the room, showing that the shot had been fired upwards from the yard below.

By now Police Constables Quint and Warboys had arrived. They made a preliminary search of the building, and found shotgun pellets both in Mr. Anstee's room and in the yard outside. Bailey gave Warboys the hammer found in the hall. They examined furniture in the house, and found much of it broken open; the tools used seemed to have been a hammer, a steel and a knife. Warboys found the steel in the drawing room.

At 6:30 a.m. Inspector Penn arrived. He too made an examination of the premises, and compared the marks on the door of Mrs. Lindsay's bedroom with the hammer. They matched.

As the day wore on the police investigation intensified. The search area was widened, and several crucial pieces of evidence came to light.

Constable Sparks found a double-barrelled shotgun in a wood just 150 yards from the house. It was a percussion muzzle-loading gun. The hammer of the left lock was down, and that barrel had recently been fired. The other hammer was on half-cock, and the barrel rusty, though dry.

Further on, items taken from Marshall's Wick Farm were found, as though discarded in haste by the fleeing murderer. Articles of clothing, a joint of mutton, and the missing plate led in the direction of Gustard's Wood to the north.

Railway workers reported that a man had been seen crossing the fields not far from Marshall's Wick at about five that morning. He had gone onto the Midland Railway line, and been reprimanded for trespass. The police followed a trail of sightings through Harpenden to the outskirts of Luton, where they lost the scent. The man was described as being about five feet five inches tall, with a sandy moustache, wearing dark clothes and a felt hat. His face was marked with small pox, and he carried a brown paper parcel.

During the day a Sandridge resident reported that he had seen Thomas Wheeler in the neighbourhood, which led the police to believe that Wheeler might be the man they were looking for. He was known to them as a suspected poacher, as were his brothers Henry and John, but none of them had any convictions for burglary or acts of violence. An order was put out for Thomas's arrest; meanwhile, at eleven that morning Superintendent Pike paid a visit to the home of Henry Wheeler at Gustard's Wood.

There they found items stolen from the burglary at Bernard's Heath, including the Snider rook rifle. Henry Wheeler, his wife Mary Anne (known as Ann) and their son George had an interesting story to tell.

At three in the morning on 9 June Tom Wheeler had come to their home and wakened them by throwing stones at the window. They had not seen him for several years, and it was some moments before they recognized him.

Henry went down and let him in. He carried with him a rough bag, which he asked Henry to look after. He did not stay long, and by the time Ann got up he was gone. That evening she found the bag in the cupboard beneath the stairs. Inside were a number of items that she suspected were stolen. She asked Henry about them, and he admitted that Tom had left them there.

Ann was extremely anxious. She wanted nothing to do with stolen goods, and told Henry so in no uncertain terms. She said she wanted them out of the house or she would report their presence to Constable Kilby.

The following morning, 10 June, at first light, Tom returned. Ann told him to take away the bag. He asked if he could leave it for a few days. No, he could not, she replied. He borrowed from her a cask and put some of the stolen goods into it. The rest stayed in the bag. He addressed them to Mrs. Wheeler, near the Black Horse, Catford, Kent. He left with both packages.

Some time later Ann found that Tom had left several items behind in the cupboard. She had no idea what to do with them; there were some glass pieces, but most worrying was the rook rifle. The glass things she put back under the stairs, and George took the rifle to his room. It was there that Superintendent Pike found it on 22 August. He also found the other pieces, which proved to be from Bernard's Heath. Henry and George Wheeler were arrested. Pike came back the following day and took Ann into custody as well. The police now had reason to believe that Tom Wheeler was responsible for the thefts from Bernard's Heath. As one of the hammers stolen from the blacksmith, William Page, was found at the scene, they also believed that Tom had stolen the hammers. The second hammer was found in the hallway of the Anstee household; therefore, it seemed probable that Tom was the killer. That the gun used came from the Woollatt robbery meant he was guilty of that burglary too. The evidence was fitting together very neatly.

On the morning of the 22 August, Tom had gone to St. Albans. The word was out that he was wanted, and several people told him so. He visited William North, and borrowed the old man's razor to shave off his moustache. He also washed some of his clothing.

The police finally tracked him down at the Pineapple public house. Just after 7 p.m. Constable Butterfield went into the taproom, where he saw Tom talking to some of the other customers. He charged him with the Bernard's Heath burglary, which he denied. Butterfield handcuffed him, and took him to the Police Station, where he further charged him with the burglaries at Samwell and Marshall's Wick Farms, and the murder of Edward Anstee. Again Tom denied the charges; he also denied having visited his brother at Gustard's Wood. Later, however, Henry's next-door-neighbour was to testify seeing him there, as did his uncle, Isaac Wheeler.

The suspect was searched, and his clothes were removed for examination. They were sent to Professor Charles Tidy at the London Hospital.

The search produced several items, including a metal ear syringe and some shot, suitable for a muzzle-loading gun. The police took the shot, along with some of those recovered from the murder scene, to a St. Albans gunsmith, George Gooch. The surgeon, Mr. Webster, provided a pellet recovered from Mr. Anstee's brain. Gooch measured and weighed all the shot, and found that they were a mixture of no. 5 and no. 6. In itself this proved little, as these sizes were, and still are, amongst the commonest in use.

During the next few days there were a number of hearings, including the committal proceedings and the adjourned inquest. A good deal of ill feeling was generated as these hearings were in camera, and the press excluded. They made several formal protests, but the only concession made by the justices was to permit them to read the depositions of the witnesses.

Murder and Misdemeanour in Hertfordshire

Eliza Coleman, Susan Lindsay and Susan Woollatt all said that Wheeler's voice was very like that of the intruder, though they could not be certain it was the same man. A few days after the murder, Mrs. Lindsay visited St. Albans Town Hall to give a description of the intruder. She was taken to a separate room, where an identity parade was held. Eight men were assembled, including Thomas Wheeler. She picked him out as the man who had entered her bedroom.

Other evidence came to light connecting Tom Wheeler with the robberies in the form of witnesses prepared to testify that he had sold them items stolen during the burglaries. Tom's explanations grew increasingly difficult to believe.

On Wednesday, 15 September, Thomas Wheeler came before the justices at St. Albans in committal proceedings for the Hertfordshire and Essex Assizes to be held in Chelmsford. The depositions of twenty-eight witnesses were read to the court; some of them called in person to clarify a few points.

Professor Tidy presented his results. There was blood on Wheeler's trousers, and it seemed to him that an attempt had been made to wash it off. He was unable to say whether it was human blood – the science of the time did not permit such fine distinctions. There were spots of blood too on his scarf and shirt. Wheeler claimed it was pig's blood.

The ear syringe found on Wheeler when he was searched at St. Albans Police Station was similar to one that Edward Anstee had used many years before, and had kept it in a cupboard in the dining room. It was one of the items taken in the burglary. An attempt was made to prove that the two syringes were one and the same, but none of the witnesses called could be certain.

Finally, two witnesses appeared to testify that Wheeler had made threats against Mr. Anstee in the past. William Lawrence, of the Rule and Compasses Inn, stated that Wheeler had said he would "do for the old bastard sooner or later." George Pearce claimed that Wheeler had told him that he would "do for bloody old Anstee." Neither of them could explain the reason for the animosity.

The magistrates believed there was a case to answer, and Thomas Wheeler was remanded in custody pending his trial. In the interim, the police continued their investigations.

On further examination, they found that the syringe had been modified. The piston was wrapped with hemp to improve its seal in the barrel. They traced George Mason, who was prepared to state under oath that he recognized the syringe as belonging to the victim; he had made the modification himself.

On Friday, 5 November the prisoner appeared before the Assize Court at Chelmsford before Sir Henry Hawkins, on a charge of the wilful murder of Edward Anstee. Mr. Talfourd Salter, Mr. Snagge and Mr. Fulton appeared for the prosecution; after some discussion, Mr. Woollett (not to be confused with the Woollatt family involved in the case) and Mr. Grubbe took on the defence. The first day began with a summary of the prosecution case, and Mr. Woollett objected to the introduction as evidence of both the hammers and the gun. They tended, he said, to prove or lead to the proof of another crime or crimes, for which the accused was not being tried. After some discussion the judge ruled that it would be wrong to exclude such evidence. Suppose one of the hammers had been used to kill Mr. Anstee? Evidence that they had been in the possession of the accused would be crucial, and it would be ridiculous to exclude it. The same went for the shotgun. This was a serious blow to the defence.

Right: Sir Henry Hawkins, judge in the case of Thomas Wheeler. From a contemporary sketch by Samuel Lucas.

The witnesses for the prosecution followed. Much of their evidence repeated that heard by the coroner and the magistrates. Some of those testifying were more certain in their statements than they had been at earlier hearings. Eliza Coleman was now sure that the voice she had heard was that of the accused. Much was made of the syringe, now that it seemed more identifiable. The judge adjourned the proceedings at 5 p.m.

The court resumed the following morning, and heard of the discovery of items stolen from Marshall's Wick Farm in fields and woods in the area, as though left behind in fleeing the scene. Susan Gray, William Little and Eleanor Chalkley described having seen Wheeler in the area on the night of the murder. The threats he had made in the past were recalled. Deputy Chief

Constable Ryder told the court of Wheeler's arrest and the subsequent events at the Police Station, which included the account Wheeler had given him at that time of his movements in the past few days.

According to Wheeler, he had left his family in Lewisham on Monday, 16 August, and went to Hatfield and Wheathampstead. On the 17th he dressed a pig for a Mrs. Matthews, thus accounting for the blood. On the Friday he spent the night on No Man's Land Common, beneath a hedge. The Saturday night he had been on Harpenden Common, some miles to the northwest of Marshall's Wick Farm.

Ann Wheeler described in detail the visits Tom had made to her home, and how he had left the stolen property there. William Page identified the hammers stolen from him, and recovered at the Beech Hyde and Marshall's Wick crime scenes. At 6 p.m. the prosecution case was complete, and the judge adjourned the court until Monday.

When the court resumed, Mr. Talfourd Salter summed up the prosecution case. Wheeler stood in the dock, looking more anxious than he had done at any time before in the proceedings.

Mr. Woollett for the defence called no witnesses, but relied upon undermining the prosecution case. He accepted that Thomas Wheeler was "a man steeped in crime," and as such they may be sure that, if they acquitted him, he would still serve a long period of penal servitude; perhaps for life. Thus Woollett hoped to give the jury an excuse to avoid responsibility in returning a "guilty" verdict likely to result in a hanging.

Woollett attempted to throw doubt on Mrs. Lindsay's identification evidence, implying that the clothing the accused was wearing was bound to make him stand out from the other men. He also attacked the identification of the syringe.

Eliza Coleman had spoken of two shots, and Mrs. Lindsay only one. Was not therefore the whole of their evidence suspect? There was no proof that the gun was ever in the possession of Thomas Wheeler, Woollett argued. The evidence was circumstantial. Nor was there any proof that the blood on Wheeler's clothes was anything other than pig's blood, as he claimed.

Sir Henry Hawkins summed up for the jury. He had a low opinion of jurymen, claiming that his dog, Jack, had more brains than any twelve jackasses to be found on the average jury. Nonetheless, he was known too for his patience, and he carefully reviewed the evidence for them. If they were not satisfied that the prisoner was guilty, he told them, they must return a "not guilty" verdict. It took them just twenty-five minutes to find Thomas Wheeler guilty of the wilful murder of Edward Anstee.

The judge told the jury that he fully agreed with their verdict. To Thomas Wheeler he said that his crime was "foul and wicked;" he had shown no remorse, but having killed Anstee, he had gone on to plunder his house. He was to be hanged by the neck until dead.

As soon as the sentence was pronounced, Wheeler fell to his knees, placing his hands on the bar at the front of the dock. He repeated the Lord's Prayer, then stood and asked to address the court. Permission was refused, and he was taken below by the warders.

That evening, after a long and earnest conversation with Mr. W. F. Lumley, the Chaplain of Springfield Gaol at Chelmsford, Wheeler confessed to the killing of Edward Anstee. His main motive was theft, he said, though he had an unspecified grudge of nine years standing against his victim. The prosecution were wrong about the syringe – it really was his. The evidence that he had most feared was not discovered; a day or two before the crime he bought powder and shot at a shop in St. Albans.

That night, with the assistance of the Chaplain, Wheeler drafted a letter to Mrs. Anstee:

H. M.'s PRISON, CHELMSFORD
Nov. 8, 1880, 10 p.m.

Mrs Anstee,

It is with heartfelt sorrow that I write you a few lines before I can sleep to-night, to beg your pardon and forgiveness for the cruel wrong I have done you. I did shoot Mr. Anstee; forgive me this great wrong. I cannot ask God's forgiveness until I have asked yours. When you tell me you have forgiven me, I shall hope that God will do the same. I have been very miserable until now; but my heart feels lighter since I have told my sin to the clergyman – through him I tell it to my fellow-men, and as I have sinned against all, I hope all will pray with me for forgiveness through the merits of our Saviour Jesus Christ. This is all my hope now. With God I must now try to make my peace. May He help me and protect my dear wife and children, and may my sin not be visited upon them with all that cruelty with which I have treated you. Pardon, I ask of you, madam. I can only say that I do wish that I had never injured you. – Believe me, your unworthy servant,

THOMAS WHEELER

Witness –   His mark X
W. F. Lumley, Chaplain

Wheeler was returned to St. Albans Gaol to await execution. There he received visits from his family and friends.

Murder and Misdemeanour in Hertfordshire

On Monday, 30 November, at 7:55 a.m., the condemned man was led from his cell in the infirmary across the prison yard to the van shed. Wheeler needed help in crossing the yard, and was clearly deeply distressed. Five members of the press were permitted to witness the punishment; others present were the Prison Governor, the Chaplain, the Surgeon and five warders. The executioner Marwood carried out the sentence of the court. He calculated the drop at eight feet eight inches. Marwood pinioned the doomed man's arms and legs, and slipped a white linen cap and the rope over his head. A moment later he pulled the bolt and Wheeler fell through the trap to his death.

As had by now become customary, the press reported that he died instantly, and that there was no sign of a struggle or convulsions. The body was left hanging for an hour before an inquest was held, and Thomas Wheeler was laid to rest within the precincts of St. Albans Gaol. His last words had been, "Do remember me to my dear wife and children – my poor dear wife and children – goodbye."

There seems little doubt that Wheeler was guilty. The case raises one matter for concern, however. Did the syringe belong to Anstee or Wheeler? If it belonged to the murdered man, then why should Wheeler lie about it after he had been convicted? Remember, at the same time he admitted buying in St. Albans the powder and shot he later used to kill Anstee, and confessed to the murder. And if the syringe belonged to Wheeler, how was it that so many witnesses managed to be certain that it was not?

Marshall's Wick Farm was pulled down just after the Second World War, and the area was swallowed by the expansion of St. Albans. Samwell's Farm, now called Samuel's Farm, still survives, looking much the same as it did over 120 years ago, when Thomas Wheeler prowled its rooms in search of plunder, and left with the gun that he later used in such a violent manner, and without warning, against the elderly farmer.

Chapter Fifteen

The Aldbury Gamekeepers, 1891

The morning of Sunday, 13 December 1891 was wet. Rain had fallen overnight, and Martin's Field behind the Stocks Estate near Aldbury was thick with mud. The field ran uphill from the Pitstone Road to the wood known as Aldbury Nowers.

By a scrubby bunch of beeches, in a pool of blood, lay the body of Joseph Crawley. A hundred yards away lay William Puddephatt. Crawley's Inverness coat was by the wood, and Puddephatt's great coat lay some forty yards further up the hill. Near Crawley was a dented gun barrel; by Puddephatt lay two pieces of broken gun stock and two sticks. There were signs of a struggle, and the footprints of three men making off in the direction of Ivinghoe.

Above: just another field... but this is where the two gamekeepers' bodies were found. (author)

It was at about 11.00 a.m. that the two men were found by the head keeper, James Double, and his helper, Charles Willmore. Double had arranged to meet Puddephatt at 10:30 that morning, and he became anxious when he did not turn up; it was unusual for Puddephatt to be late. Double walked through Howlett's Wood, finding to his surprise that the corn bins for the pheasant feed had not been touched - Puddephatt always fed the birds.

Looking down across the field, he saw what he thought at first was a log; when he saw a second form, he began to fear the worst.

He checked Crawley first. The man was clearly dead. He lay on his front, with his hands raised to his face. Puddephatt was on his back, partially turned to one side, with one arm outstretched. Double took his hand - it was cold.

Above: the Greyhound Inn in Aldbury, where the bodies of William Puddephatt and Joseph Crawley were taken on the morning of Sunday, 13th December 1891. (author)

Having established that the two men were dead, Double sent Willmore to contact the police at Tring, while he himself went to give information to Police Constable Best at Aldbury. Best had only been in the village for a month, but he knew what had to be done. He sent his wife to the Reverend Wood, to ask him to let the victims' wives know what had happened before they heard it by rumour; whilst he, Double and several other men returned to the scene of the killings. They arranged for the bodies to be taken to the Greyhound Public House in the centre of Aldbury, where the inquest was to be held the following evening. Care was taken to disturb the scene as little as possible.

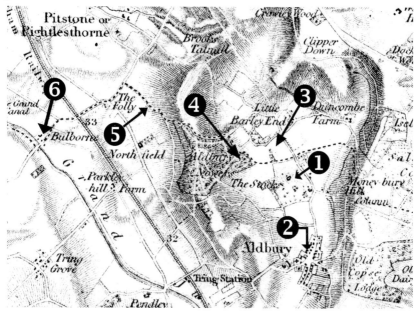

Above: 1 – Stocks House; 2 – the Greyhound, Aldbury; 3 – the field in which Puddephatt and Crawley were found; 4 - Howlett's Wood; 5 – the Hertford-shire/Buckinghamshire border; 6 – Bulbourne (spelled Bulborne on this map), on the Grand Union Canal. (courtesy Ordnance Survey).

William Puddephatt was a professional gamekeeper of many years standing. He was 37 years old, married, with five children. He was of muscular build, and known as a determined and courageous man. Joseph Crawley was five years older than Puddephatt. He was employed as a night-watchman, a job he had held for only ten months. Before that, he had been a farm labourer. He left a wife and seven children in the village of Aldbury. On the night in question he had been assigned to work with Puddephatt.

It became clear before the inquest that this would be a case of joint jurisdiction between Hertfordshire and Buckinghamshire police. The bodies had been found two hundred yards inside Buckinghamshire, but had been carried over the border into Aldbury. In the event, none of the administrative problems that might have been anticipated arose.

On Monday, senior officers from Buckinghamshire Police took charge of the crime scene. Casts were taken of the footprints, and the area searched. They believed that Puddephatt and Crawley had come upon three poachers, and in the ensuing struggle, both of the men had been killed. It was to be expected that the poachers would have received some form of injury during the fight.

Double had already told the police that only a week earlier shots had been heard coming from the direction of the Stocks Estate. As a result he and Puddephatt had been taking turns to watch the area at night. On the night of 12 December, at about 10.30 p.m., Double had met Puddephatt and Crawley in the lane leading to the Estate. Alfred Pike, a coachman, had volunteered to accompany Puddephatt and Crawley on their rounds. Unfortunately his coach duties intervened, and they had gone without him. We can only speculate on the course of events had he been there to help.

Double was able to confirm to the police that the two men had been carrying sticks, but no firearms.

The police already had their suspicions as to who they were looking for. Their names were Walter Smith, Frederick Eggleton and Charles Rayner. They were known poachers, and at about 10.00 p.m. on the night in question they had been seen drinking at Bulbourne in the Grand Junction Arms, a public house not far from the Stocks Estate. Constable Best searched Rayner's home on Sunday 13 December, but he was not there; however, Best found a pair of wet, bloodstained trousers. The following day the indefatigable Best found two hats and two powder flasks near the scene of the crime.

The flasks indicate that at least one, and possibly both, of the poachers' guns was muzzle-loading, rather than using cartridges. This may explain why Crawley and Puddephatt were not shot. Muzzle-loading guns are susceptible to wet weather, and on a night like the 12 December, they might not have fired. Though such guns were obsolete by 1891, their use continued in rural areas well into the 20th century.

On Monday 14 December Walter Smith was arrested on suspicion, but the other two men were still missing from their homes in Tring.

On that same Monday evening the inquest was held at the Greyhound. Double told of the discovery of the bodies, and their removal to the Greyhound, and a surgeon, Mr. Edward Le Queen, who had examined the bodies at the scene, gave medical evidence, describing the injuries the two men had suffered.

Puddephatt he found lying on his back with his right arm outstretched. There was a large wound across the nose and beyond the left orbit, smashing the bones of the upper jaw. The left eye was ruptured, and there was a wound 2½ inches above the right eye. There was a star wound with a small depressed fracture of the skull. The whole of the left side of the skull had been smashed by repeated blows, and the right arm broken. Some at least of the blows to the head had been struck as Puddephatt lay on the ground. In Le Queen's opinion the victim had been stunned, then beaten to death as he lay helpless. The wounds could have been inflicted with a gun barrel, the small projection of the bead fore sight of which might have caused the star-shaped indentation.

Crawley was lying on his face with his hands raised. There was a large wound to the left base of the skull, from which the brain protruded. Detached portions of the skull adhered to the scalp. There had been more than one blow, and there were two other large wounds to the base of the skull. Le Queen concluded that Crawley had been struck from behind, and that he too had received further blows as he lay on the ground. The inquest was adjourned until Monday, 18 January.

Further enquiries revealed the movements of the three suspects on the night in question. On Saturday 12 December all three men had been drinking in the Queen's Arms in Tring from about 8.00 p.m., and had stayed about an hour. The landlord, Fred Philby, had lent Eggleton a gun. From the Queen's Arms the three men went to the Grand Junction Arms, where they had more beer, and some bread and cheese.

On the night following the murders Eggleton and Rayner had been seen by a boatman throwing something into the canal at Bulbourne. The canal was dragged, and the stock of a gun found.

Smith had been taken into custody the following morning, but Rayner and Eggleton had fled. They went to the house of Rayner's father at Buckland Common, where Eggleton said to Rayner's brother David, "I don't know whether they (Puddephatt and Crawley) are dead or alive. I should like to know if they have got Walt (Walter Smith)."

Where they went from there is not known, but their trail was picked up again from Friday 18 December. They were arrested at Watlington by Sergeant Yates of the Oxfordshire Police; but he was not sure of their identity, so he released them. Unsurprisingly when he returned to re-arrest them, they had moved on.

They next called on Samuel Jenning at Denne Hill. They asked to sleep there, and whether there were any police in the area. Rayner said, "We killed one man, and don't know how the other gets on." The next morning they left, saying they were heading for "the Smoke" (London).

They were finally apprehended by Sergeant Payne on 21 December, near a stable at Denham. A police doctor examined them, and found bruises and wounds that indicated they had recently been involved in a fight.

It must have come as a shock to them to learn that while they had been on the run, Smith had made a statement. He admitted that he had been in the woods that night, and that he had seen Puddephatt and Crawley on the ground. He denied having been involved in their murder.

All three men appeared at the Magistrates' court at Ivinghoe, and were remanded in custody.

On 23 January 1892, the inquest reconvened. After some minor points of clarification, the jury returned a verdict of wilful murder against Walter Smith, Frederick Eggleton and Charles Rayner.

The trial took place on 23 February 1892 at Buckinghamshire Assizes at Aylesbury. The jury heard the evidence given in the committal proceedings. All three men admitted being in the woods for the purpose of poaching, but claimed that they had been attacked by Puddephatt and Crawley. It did them no good. Eggleton and Rayner were found guilty of murder and sentenced to death; Smith was found guilty of manslaughter, and given twenty years penal servitude. The execution date for Eggleton and Rayner was set for Tuesday 17 March, to be carried out at Oxford Gaol.

The mood of much of the public now swayed in their favour. Pleas for mercy appeared in the newspapers, variously claiming that

- the fight had taken place when passions on both sides were aroused
- the keepers had struck the first blows
- the poachers were acting at least partially in self-defence
- no-one but those concerned could know what had really happened.

Finally, it was argued that it would be unfair upon the wives and children of the condemned men to taint them with the gallows stigma for the rest of their lives.

A petition for their reprieve was sent to the Home Secretary. In the meantime, they continued to assert that the deaths of Puddephatt and Crawley had been an unfortunate result of the fight between the poachers and gamekeepers. There had, they maintained, been no intention to kill.

One of the jurors wrote to the Home Secretary, saying that he and some of the others had wanted to return a verdict of manslaughter, but the majority had thought otherwise. After some argument, the supporters of the lesser verdict had capitulated on the grounds that they were out-voted.

The Home Secretary came under pressure in the House of Commons, but stood firm. The gamekeepers had been brutally murdered, and the medical evidence was that they were struck either from behind or as they lay helpless upon the ground. The conclusion must be that there had been a deliberate intention either seriously to injure, or to kill, Crawley and Puddephatt as they lay defenceless. The guilty men would hang.

The condemned men's wives visited them at 10.00 a.m. on the morning of 16 March, and it fell to Eggleton and Rayner themselves to tell them that the appeal for clemency had been rejected.

Three members of the press were permitted to report on the execution. Mr. Billington, of Bolton, was engaged to carry out the sentence of the court. The procession was headed by the prison chaplain, reading the Burial Service. Rayner followed, wearing his working clothes, and a deerstalker hat. Then came several warders, Eggleton, the executioner and the prison officials. The men were placed on the gallows, the ropes positioned and the bolt pulled. The drop for Rayner was calculated at 7 feet, as he was the taller of the two; that for Eggleton was 6 feet 9 inches. Both men repeated the responses to the Burial Service throughout. The newspapers reported that death appeared instantaneous.

Between them the three offenders had three wives and fifteen children. The murdered men's dependants numbered two wives and twelve children.

The total: four men dead and thirty-two people unprovided for, and all for the sake of a few pheasants, none of which belonged to the people whose lives were devastated by the events of that tragic December night.

Chapter Sixteen

The Assault on Sarah Dye, Goose Green, Hoddesdon, 1891

Sarah Dye was only fourteen years old, and lived with her parents in Hertford. In the early evening of Sunday 12 July 1891 she went for a walk out towards Hoddesdon with her friend, Nelly Noads. With them went two young men, named Wren and Cooper.

By the time the companions reached Goose Green, some three or four miles away, they were thirsty, and they stopped at the Green Man public house for some ginger beer. They noticed a number of men sitting on a bench outside the pub.

Above: The Green Man at Goose Green, just outside Hoddesdon. It is now called the Huntsman. Some of those accused of the assault were sitting in front of this pub when Sarah and her friends arrived. (author)

Sarah and her friends left at about 8.45 p.m., and started back for Hertford. They decided to cross the stile into Box Wood, but as they did so seven or

108

eight men came towards them. They knocked Wren down. The four young people retreated to the pub, the men following them.

Wren, Cooper and Nelly Noads made off, leaving Sarah to make her way home to Hertford alone. Why the others left her by herself is a mystery, but as far as Sarah was concerned, it was to prove a disastrous move.

The group of men followed her, and after about a quarter of a mile 16-year-old Joseph Nottage grabbed her around the waist. With the aid of some of the others he dragged her to the ground. Frederick Faint, also aged 16, then assaulted her while others, including 37-year-old James Wells, held her down. By now about a dozen men had gathered to watch the proceedings. Sarah was heard to cry, "Mother, mother!" One of the men put his hand over her mouth to prevent her calling out again.

After this assault the men released her, and she started for home once more. She did not get far. A little way down the road the men seized her again. They pulled the skirt of her dress off, dragged her to a secluded spot behind a hedge, and Wells assaulted her while seven or eight others stood and watched. Sarah fainted.

When she recovered consciousness she dressed and once more set off for home. Wells followed her for some distance, and at one point got hold of her again, but she escaped. She arrived in Hertford at about 11.00 p.m. She said nothing to her parents, but on the Wednesday following she went to Hoddesdon Police Station and reported the assault.

Over the next few days she identified several of men involved, some at Hoddesdon Police Station, some at Hertford.

In August, Faint, Wells and Nottage appeared before the Summer Sessions of Hertford Assizes. Faint pleaded guilty, but Wells and Nottage denied the charges. A number of other men absconded and did not appear in court.

Several witnesses were called, including Mark Frost of Hertford, who testified that at different times six of the group of men had assaulted Sarah. Some claimed that they had attempted to come to Sarah's aid, but were unable to do so because so many men were involved. Robert Miles had attempted to intervene, and had been punched in the eye for his interference.

Mr. H. S. W. Hall, a Hertford surgeon, gave medical evidence. He said that he had examined Sarah on 16 July, and found evidence that a serious assault had taken place.

Witnesses appeared for the defence, claiming that whilst Nottage had been at the scene, he had not been involved; others implied, Nottage amongst them, that Sarah had been a willing party to the evening's entertainment. According to him, Sarah asked him to show her the road back to Hertford. They walked a short distance, and he saw that several men were following. He said, "Who do you want out of all the lot of us?" "You," she replied, and took his arm. A short while later, the other men rushed up and seized Sarah, so Nottage went home.

Wells said that he had seen the assault and heard Sarah scream. He had remonstrated with those taking part; they rounded on him, so he had gone back to the Green Man for some more beer. When he returned he found Sarah in the process of being assaulted for the second time.

The defence for Nottage told the jury that they were not being asked to try the young man for cowardice or being a blackguard; but for aiding and abetting others in a serious assault on a young girl. There were many others present that evening guilty of more serious crimes than Nottage, but they were not before the court. Presumably the defence felt that it was unfair to try only those who had surrendered to their bail.

Nonetheless the jury found Wells guilty of criminal assault and Nottage guilty of indecent assault. Wells was sentenced to ten years' penal servitude; Nottage got nine months. Faint, who had pleaded guilty, was given five years.

The judge was particularly scathing in his condemnation of Wells. A man of thirty-seven, he said, might reasonably be expected to protect a young girl like Sarah. Instead he joined the others in assaulting her.

Before closing the case, the judge had some strong words for the lads who had given evidence on behalf of Nottage. Some of them had lied, he told them, and lying in court was perjury, punishable by up to seven years' imprisonment. They had come very close to being sent down for their distortion of the truth.

Perhaps one of the more revealing statements about the attitudes of the period was made by Sarah herself, as she lay on the ground following the first assault. "You had better let me get up," she said, "because if my father was to know it I should get a good thrashing."

She showed a great deal of courage in reporting the offence, knowing that she would face the humiliation of a public trial and the stigma that would attach to her for the rest of her life.

Chapter Seventeen

"Rotten" Smith and Mercy Nicholls, Hertford, 1899

The year 1899 was remarkable in Hertfordshire for two sensational murders. They shocked the county, but for entirely different reasons. Both deaths occurred within a couple of days of each other, and both of the accused were tried at the same Summer Assizes at Hertford in that year.

The first of these crimes was brutal in the extreme, but it was the behaviour of both the police and townspeople of Hertford that attracted as much condemnation as the murderer himself.

Mercy Carter was twenty-one years old when she married Samuel Nicholls, a brickmaker, in 1893. They set up home in Baldock Street in Ware. After the first three years the match does not seem to have been a happy one. There had been a number of disturbances in the household, and Samuel had struck his wife on several occasions. There had been more than one separation in the past. Sometime about the middle of February the couple parted again, and Mercy went home to her mother at Cole's Green in Suffolk. On 7 March 1899 she left her mother with the intention of returning to her husband at Ware.

By 8 March she had reached Hertford. She got no further, for she fell into company with an illegitimate cousin of hers, John Smith, whose age was variously given as seventeen, eighteen and nineteen. It is quite possible that he did not know how old he was himself. Smith was small for his age, and not over-bright. He was known to some by the nickname "Rotten," and was waiting to join the militia. No one who knew him would have suspected he was capable of the dreadful violence he displayed in the early hours of the following morning in Railway Street.

Though the exact movements of the couple that evening are difficult to trace, some details are recorded. At 10:45 p.m. they called on Susan Maynard, Smith's aunt; she later testified that, whilst Smith was sober, Mercy was "the worse for drink." Smith told her that they were going to look for lodgings. At midnight they were seen talking in Railway Street.

Where they went and what they did for the next two and a half hours is a mystery; but at 2:25 a.m. Jane Papper, whose husband Charles was the local lamplighter, heard a woman screaming loudly, "Good God, am I dying? Is there no water anywhere?" She lay listening for a while, and even got out of bed, but could see nothing through the curtain of heavy rain that was falling. She thought little of the matter; as she said later, "we hear so many rows." She did not think it her duty to investigate further.

At half past three Francis Burton, of 9, Railway Street, a town councillor, heard cries of "Help" and "Police." He opened his window, and saw a woman on the ground. He watched the proceedings for a quarter of an hour before going back to bed. He later said that he "thought they were two tramps... We often get disturbances in the street – only the previous Christmas a man had his leg broken there."

About the same time John Smith knocked at the door of Frederick and Elizabeth Davis. When Mrs. Davis opened the window he asked her for the loan of an axe to "chop a woman's head off." When she asked, "what woman?" Smith dragged Mercy Nicholls from the shadows outside the Young Men's Christian Association rooms and dropped her in the gutter.

Alfred Wright, a stockman, and his son Ebenezer came into Railway Street. Mrs. Davis called to him and asked him to get the police. Ebenezer said to Wright, "That's Rotten, father." Wright saw Mercy in the gutter, and noticed that Smith had something in his hand that glinted in the lamplight. He realised it was a knife.

Smith called out, "The Prince of Wales has got no money; Queen Victoria has got all the money." Then, as Mrs. Davis watched, he pulled Mercy up by her arms and dropped her. Then he kicked her, twice.

Wright hurried off to get the police, leaving Ebenezer behind to follow Smith if he left the scene. The lad stood at the street corner, from which he saw Smith drag Mercy into the yard of the Diamond, where he kicked her again. Wright senior returned. He had gone to the Police Station in nearby Queen Street, arriving there at about 3:40 a.m., where he had spoken to Police Constable Sherwood and told him that a man was "killing a woman in the street." Sherwood replied, "I can't leave the station until another constable comes in. I expect one in in a minute. I will go at once then." Believing that Mercy was already dead, and that a constable would arrive at any moment, Wright and his boy went on their way. As they passed the Hertford Union, they heard the clock strike four.

As the stockman heard the clock strike, Charles Papper, the lamplighter, arrived in Railway Street. It was his wife Jane that had done nothing when she heard Mercy being assaulted an hour and a half earlier. Papper saw Smith marching up and down in the street. He had seen him with Mercy late the previous night, but now he seemed to be alone. When he returned about twenty minutes later, he saw Mercy lying in the gutter outside Elliot's bakers.

He saw that she had been stabbed, and she called out, "Help!" several times. Incredibly, Papper did nothing to come to her aid, and continued on his round. Job Edwards, Papper's supervisor, saw Smith marching up Parliament Row and into Maidenhead Street, calling out, "left, right" as he did so. Edwards met Papper a few minutes later, at about 4:20 a.m. Papper told him that there was an almost naked woman lying in Railway Street. "Did you help her?" asked Edwards. "No," replied Papper, "they are gypsies." He said that he had not wanted to interfere for fear of being stabbed. Edwards told him to fetch the police, but Papper refused and went off on his rounds. Disgusted, Edwards went to the Police Station himself, where he reported the matter to P.C. Sherwood. The constable told him he was waiting for P.C. Langstone.

At a quarter past five Papper told Frederick Ashman about the assault, and admitted that he had done nothing. He had, he said, his lamps to put out. Ashman went straight to the Police Station, where he reported the assault to the constable on duty. The officer promised to send Langstone as soon as he arrived.

Charles Bailey had arrived at the Diamond Yard after having been told that there was a woman lying there. He gathered some of her clothes, and covered her. He stayed with Mercy until Edwards returned at about 5:30 a.m. She mumbled, "Oh, Jack." Edwards tried unsuccessfully to find some sacks to cover the injured woman. He told Bailey about his trip to the Police Station, and Bailey decided to report the assault yet again, arriving there a few minutes later. On being told that the woman was seriously injured, Sherwood at last woke Constable Hewitt, the constable who lived at the station, and a few minutes later the two officers started for Railway Street, carrying a stretcher.

By now it was almost six o'clock, and Hertford was waking up. More passers by made their way into Railway Street, including, at five minutes to six, James Saunders. He saw Mercy covered with blood, such that he could not tell whether she was "a white woman or a black one." A moment later the two constables finally arrived at the scene. As Saunders looked around he spotted a knife, lying in a pool of blood. He picked it up and gave it to a constable. He was able to identify the weapon by marks on the handle and the broken tip of the blade.

The constables carried Mercy to the Infirmary, where she died soon after 10 a.m. from loss of blood and hypothermia.

John Smith meanwhile had gone to the Coachmakers' Arms lodging house, where he went into the room of John Brown. Brown awoke, and asked Smith what he wanted; he made no reply, and started down the stairs. Brown followed him and the two men struggled on the stairs. Brown overpowered Smith, and took him to the kitchen, where he found another lodger, Thomas Montagu. The three men sat around the table talking.

A short time later James Saunders came in and told them that "a poor woman has copped it in Back Street" (the old name for Railway Street). Smith said "I done it." Saunders asked him if he still had the knife, but Smith said he had lost it. Brown sent Saunders for the police. While Saunders was on his way to the Police Station, Brown asked Smith to show him where the assault had happened. Smith, Brown and Montagu made their way to Railway Street, where Smith pointed to a pool of blood and said, "That is where I left my knife." Indicating the Diamond archway, he said, "That is where the Prince of Wales died." Brown, in company with Montagu, took Smith to the Police Station, arriving there at 6:40 a.m., and handed him over to Constable George Hart, who took him into custody.

At the inquest on 11 March the full horror of Mercy's injuries came to light. Dr. William Roach told the court that Mercy had been stabbed no less than fifty-nine times.

Most of the injuries were to her head, throat and arms, though there were four to the chest and two to the abdomen. There was extensive bruising to the knees, spine, forehead and chin. None of the injuries was enough to kill her however; the cause of death was loss of blood and exposure. Had Mercy been brought to the infirmary two hours earlier, he said, she would undoubtedly have made a full recovery. Dr. Roach's testimony amounted to a condemnation of the police, and those people who witnessed the assault but had done nothing to help the injured woman. The hearing was adjourned.

The furore over the callous behaviour of many of the onlookers, and the failure of the police to act quickly, speedily grew. On 13 March the County Council met, and H. R. H. Gosselin, the Mayor of Hertford, raised the matter. Would there, he wanted to know, be a full investigation into the conduct of the police? Indeed there would, he was assured.

On 20 March the inquest resumed. Constable Sherwood denied having been summoned to the scene several times. The first he knew of the assault was at half past four, he claimed, when Alfred Wright had called in. Nothing in that initial report led him to believe that the matter was serious. He had been alone in the station and unable to leave it (this was untrue – PC Hewitt and the local Superintendent had been asleep upstairs). It was not until Bailey reported the assault that he realised anything of significance had occurred. He had then roused Hewitt, and they had got the ambulance ready to take Mercy to the Infirmary. His claim that Wright had not come to the station until 4:30 a.m. was queried, but he was adamant. Wright was recalled to the witness box. He was just as certain that he had spoken to Sherwood at 3:30 a.m.

The beat officer, Constable Langstone, said that he had been out on his beat all night and heard nothing. He had finished his duty at six o'clock and gone straight home without visiting the Police Station to book out.

The Coroner said in his summing up that he did not believe either Sherwood or Langstone. There was an implication that there had been an arrangement between the two men, and that either Langstone had not been on duty at all, or, if he had, that he had gone home early. The jury returned a verdict of wilful murder against John Smith with the following rider: "We consider the conduct of Police Constables Langstone and Sherwood as deserving of the severest censure, and their evidence not to be relied on."

John Smith was scheduled to appear before the Borough Bench of Magistrates on Thursday, 16 March, but it was clear that he was unfit, both physically and mentally, to plead. Indeed, the prison doctors provided a certificate to that effect. Lieutenant-Colonel Daniell, the Chief Constable, told the Bench that he understood the boy to be in a state of complete collapse. By 23 March he had recovered sufficiently to be brought by train from St. Albans to Hertford, where he was held in the cells at the Shire Hall.

When he appeared before the magistrates, he appeared uninterested. He sat on a chair in the dock, and gazed vacantly out of the window, open-mouthed. From time to time he looked at the two constables flanking him, but showed no emotion as the details of the charge against him were recounted.

When he spoke, what little he said made no sense. He made several references to the Prince of Wales and Queen Victoria "being on the other side." When charged with the murder, Smith pointed to one of the policemen and said, "He's my brother." He was committed for trial at Hertford Assizes.

The newspapers condemned the two constables, Sherwood and Langstone, and the lamplighter Charles Papper, in the strongest terms. Those who had seen and heard the attack, and done nothing about it, were also targets of censure. So too was Chief Constable Daniell, for some remarks he made at the inquest disparaging some of the witnesses, one of whom he referred to as "a cowardly sneak."

With the exception of Daniell, all of the people the press vilified received threats and insults as they went about their lives. The Secretary of State for the Home Department was asked in Parliament whether criminal proceedings would be brought against Sherwood and Langstone.

Early in May the committee of inquiry requested by Mr. Gosselin, the mayor, released its report. Its findings came under seven headings:

1. The committee was satisfied that Constables Langstone and Sherwood were negligent. Langstone had either left his beat early, or had not patrolled it properly. Sherwood had been informed at least twice that a serious incident was occurring in Railway Street, but he did not go to investigate, nor did he inform his Superintendent or Constable Hewitt, both of whom were resident at

the Police Station and asleep upstairs. Speaking tubes were installed between the guardroom and the bedrooms, so there was no excuse for failing to do so. The committee approved the dismissal of both men.

2. The committee impressed upon the Chief Constable the importance of constables reporting serious incidents to their superior officer straight away.

3. Supervision of constables on the beat was inadequate. They should be checked upon at irregular intervals to ensure that they performed their duties with diligence. Diaries of such checks should be maintained, and submitted at regular intervals to the Chief Constable.

4. An attendance book should be kept, and properly completed, recording the times every constable came on and went off duty.

5. The beat that included Railway Street was too large; it was possible for the beat constable to be as far as a mile away. The district had a large number of lodging houses and a shifting population, and was known for rowdiness and disorderly conduct. A constable should always be within easy reach of the area. The extent of the beat should be reduced, especially at night.

Right: Lt. Col. Henry Smith Daniell, Chief Constable of Hertfordshire Constabulary at the time of the murder of Mercy Nicholls. His remarks made during the inquest were not appreciated in some quarters.

6. Either a Sergeant or a Superintendent should inspect the lodging houses in the area nightly. They should report on whether there was rowdy behaviour or overcrowding.
7. The complement of the Hertford station should be increased by one officer.

The Summer Assizes opened on Wednesday 28 June. It tried a calendar of unusually serious offences: two murders, two attempted murders, a case of night poaching, two arsons, one embezzlement, an attempted suicide, a criminal assault, a burglary and three cases of common theft.

The Grand Jury, at the direction of the judge, Mr. Justice Mathew, found a true bill, and committed Smith for trial. His case came up on the first day.

There was no doubt that Smith had killed Mercy Nicholls. He had been seen assaulting her; his clothes were bloodstained; and he had admitted it. The question the court had to answer was whether he had been sane at the time of the offence.

Mr. Grubbe for the prosecution stated at the outset that there was some doubt as to Smith's sanity, and as his first witnesses he wished call Dr. Boycott of Hertfordshire County Lunatic Asylum. Dr. Boycott had examined Smith on three occasions. With the judge's agreement, a jury was sworn in to try Smith on his fitness to plead.

Dr. Boycott testified that he believed Smith to be insane and suffering from delusions. He was incapable of understanding the proceedings of the court. There was insanity in the family, with two members in the asylum, and a history of inter-marriage between cousins.

The jury took only moments to find John Smith unfit to plead. Mr. Justice Mathew ordered him to be detained during her Majesty's pleasure, and he was sent to Broadmoor Criminal Lunatic Asylum.

Why did John Smith kill Mercy Nicholls? The real motive was never revealed. The boy seems to have been suffering from some sort of obsession with the Prince of Wales and Queen Victoria, though the nature of it is not clear from the records we have of his ramblings.

The verdict of the court was a just one, however. Smith was a danger to the public at large, and had to be confined both for their safety and his own.

Chapter Eighteen

The Poisoned Cake: Caroline Ansell Watford, 1899

The second of the two Hertfordshire murders in March 1899 was that of Caroline Ansell, a woman of twenty-six. She had been an inmate at the Metropolitan Asylum for Imbeciles at Leavesden, near Watford, for a number of years. According to her father, she had been quite normal until her brother had been killed in an accident. She "fretted so much that her mind gave way," he said. Her parents lived in Somers Town, and visited her from time to time. A sister, Mary Ann Ansell, aged twenty-two, was in service with the Malony family at number 42, Great Coram Street, Bloomsbury.

Right: the unfortunate victim, Caroline Ansell, who was poisoned at the Metropolitan Asylum near Watford. From a contemporary newspaper cutting.

On 22 February 1899 a package arrived at the asylum addressed to Caroline. It contained tea and Demerara sugar. When Caroline and her fellow inmates tried the tea the following morning, they found it very black, with a bitter and

unpleasant flavour. On the advice of the nurse, Alice Falmingham, they threw it away.

Later the same day nurse Falmingham found Caroline in tears. When questioned, she showed the nurse a letter she had just received: it was no wonder she was deeply upset. The letter was short and to the point, and was signed with the name Harriet Parish, one of Caroline's cousins. It ran as follows:

> Dear Carrie,
> I now send these few lines to tell you that your mother and father is dead. I am very sorry for you and the dear ones that are left. All the children send their love to you, and hope that you are quite well.

Though Caroline was in an asylum for imbeciles, she was quite literate. She wrote to her cousin asking for details. The letter caused consternation when it was passed on to her parents, who were very much alive. Mrs. Ansell immediately wrote back, reassuring her daughter that the letter was a cruel hoax. She asked Caroline to send the forged letter to her, which the girl duly did.

On 9 March Caroline received a second package, wrapped in brown paper, containing a small cake. There seemed little remarkable about it other than its bright yellow filling.

During the evening of 10 March Caroline ate about half of it, giving the rest to other inmates: Mary Smithers, Mary Driscoll, and Mary and Kate Maloney. Kate found the taste bitter and unpleasant, and spat her portion out. The others ate theirs over the next twenty-four hours.

The following morning Caroline complained of feeling unwell, and the whites of her eyes had taken on a yellowish hue. Nonetheless she went about her daily tasks as usual. By lunchtime though she was worse, and Nurse Falmingham gave her "a piece of dry toast and a black draught." The girl was sick. The other women, with the exception of Kate Maloney, suffered similar symptoms, though to a lesser degree.

On the 12 March Caroline seemed much better, but two days later she suffered a relapse. She was clearly seriously ill. She complained of acute abdominal pain, and the duty doctor had her transferred to the infirmary. Her lips, face and eyes were discoloured. Caroline attributed her illness to the cake she had eaten; Dr. Elkins, the medical superintendent, and Dr. Blair, his assistant, suspected peritonitis. Throughout the day her condition worsened, and at 6 p.m. she lost consciousness. Two hours later, she died.

The cause of death was confused by an outbreak of typhoid at the hospital. Some of the symptoms of that disease were similar to Caroline's illness, but there were differences. Dr. Elkins could find no evidence of peritonitis, and he became suspicious. He thought that the dead woman showed signs of irritant poisoning.

The Asylum wrote to Caroline's parents informing them of the death, and Mrs. Ansell and Mary visited the hospital on 16 March. Mary especially seemed very upset. Dr. Blair interviewed Mrs. Ansell. He told her that as Caroline had died somewhat suddenly, and it had come to his notice that she had eaten part of a cake sent to her, he would like to carry out a post mortem. Mrs. Ansell gave her provisional permission, but said that she would have to consult with her husband.

When the two women got home, Mary raised the matter of the post mortem with her father. She urged him to refuse permission; as a consequence he dictated a letter to that effect, which Mary wrote down. The hospital received it the following day.

By now it had become clear that Caroline had exhibited the classic symptoms of phosphorous poisoning. Initially there is nausea and vomiting. The victim then enjoys two or three days of apparently good health, which is followed by a rapid decline and death. The post mortem therefore went ahead, carried out by Dr. A. E. Cox. Sure enough, he found evidence of phosphorous, and the police were called.

On 18 March Superintendent Wood and Sergeant Peck went to the asylum. They took statements from a number of those involved and impounded several documents. They also took possession of four jars containing Caroline's organs, which were sent to Dr. Thomas Stevenson, doctor of forensic medicine at Guy's Hospital in London. His initial examination concurred with Dr. Cox's opinion; further tests confirmed it.

Superintendent Wood had a murder on his hands. Someone had sent Caroline a cake poisoned with phosphorous. The same person had presumably sent the tea and sugar, which were almost certainly poisoned too. Did the same person send the letter telling Caroline that her parents were dead? If so, why?

It was clearly important to gather all the evidence available. Wood organized a search of the asylum rubbish tip in order to trace the packaging in which the cake arrived. He was lucky. Against all the odds, Constable Thomas Piggott found the wrapping paper.

Officers compared the handwriting on the packaging, the letter claiming that Caroline's parents were dead, and the letter refusing permission for a post mortem. They thought there was a similarity, so they consulted Thomas Gurrin, a handwriting expert. In his opinion all the samples were by the same hand. The post mortem letter was known to have been written by Mary Ansell, so Wood now had a suspect for the murder: the victim's sister. What he now needed to establish was a motive.

Further enquiries revealed that Mary was engaged to be married, and she had set the date for Easter of that year. Her fiancé was less sure; he felt that they did not have enough money to set up home yet, and he preferred to wait until they had. Mary needed money.

On 6 September 1898, she approached John Cooper, the agent for the Royal London Friendly Society, who regularly visited her employers to collect premiums, with a proposal to insure Caroline's life. She wanted, she said, to be able to give her sister a proper burial when she died. Even though Caroline was only twenty-six years old, Cooper did not think to query Mary's reason for wanting the insurance.

The policy was written for £22 10s. There were conditions attached: if Caroline died within six months of the effective date, only one third of the sum assured would be paid. If death occurred between six months and a year, only half would be due. On the proposal, Mary stated that Caroline was a general servant at the Watford Asylum, and in good health. The premium was three pence a week.

The police made visits to shops in the Bloomsbury area, and again they struck lucky. Emily Noakes, whose father was an "oil and colourman," knew Mary Ansell well; she had sold her four or five penny bottles of phosphor paste that year. Mary had told her that she wanted it to poison rats.

Mrs. Malony told the officers that she had never asked Mary to buy rat poison. She had occasionally heard rats in the house, but had always set traps, never poison. She further revealed that Mary slept in the front kitchen of the house, and would have had ample opportunity to bake a cake.

Superintendent Wood decided that the time had come to arrest Mary Ansell for the murder of her sister. Among her effects was a bottle containing the phosphorous-based rat poison. On analysis it was found to contain enough phosphorous to kill three people.

Mary appeared twice before the magistrates at Watford Police Court. On the second occasion her mother became overwrought, as well she might, and had a fit of hysterics. The hearing was adjourned for lunch, and as there were no cells at the court, Mary walked the two hundred yards back to the Police Station in company with several constables and a female warder. On their return Mrs. Ansell waylaid them, and threw herself into her Mary's arms, crying "Oh, my daughter, my daughter!" Both women wept bitterly, and it was some seconds before they could be separated.

On 20 June 1899, Mary Ansell was tried for her life at Hertford Assizes before Mr. Justice Mathew. Mr. J. Rawlinson Q.C. and Mr. Grubbe conducted the prosecution, and Mr. W. Clarke Hall and Mr. Theobald Mathew appeared for the defence.

Murder and Misdemeanour in Hertfordshire

The prosecution case was clear. Mary had the opportunity and the motive. She had written the false letter so that following Caroline's death the asylum authorities would not contact her parents, believing them dead. Her handwriting was on the paper that the cake had been wrapped in. She had lied to the insurance agent about her sister's occupation. Finally, she had bought poison on several occasions, and indeed still had some in her possession. The defence attacked the medical evidence, suggesting that the cause of death had not been poison at all, but "acute yellow atrophy of the liver."

The examination of the prosecution witnesses took up the whole of the first day of the trial. The jury spent the night in the Assembly Room of the Shire Hall.

On the morning of Friday 30 June Mr. Clarke Hall called Mary to the stand to testify in her own defence.

Right: Mary Ann Ansell in the dock at Hertford Assizes, as depicted in the Penny Illustrated Paper *in 1899.*

She denied that the writing in the Parish letter and on the wrapping paper were hers. She had, she admitted, bought the poison, and that Mrs. Maloney had not known about it. She said that when she reported the rat problem, nothing was done. She had therefore taken matters into her own hands. She had pushed the poison into the rat holes with a stick, and whilst she could not say for certain that she had killed any rats, she had detected a smell that suggested to her that she had had some success.

It was true that she had insured her sister's life, but she had made no secret of it; in fact she had told Mrs. Maloney all about it. She was not short of money. The only reason she had not claimed her sister's body at the asylum was that they seemed anxious to retain it due to the unusual circumstances of her death. At the interview with Dr. Blair he had spoken of a cake, about which she knew nothing.

Mr. Rawlinson for the prosecution addressed the jury. There were two points for them to consider. Firstly, was Caroline's death caused by poison, or, as the defence had suggested, by natural causes? If they found that poison was the cause, then they must decide whether the defendant was responsible for administering the poison. There was, he suggested, little doubt as to the cause of Caroline's death. He reiterated the prosecution evidence, and in conclusion said that if the jury accepted the prosecution evidence, they could come to no other conclusion than that Caroline had been poisoned, that the poison was in the cake, and that Mary Ansell was responsible.

Mr. Clarke Hall for the defence attacked the likelihood of the prosecution case. Was it likely, he asked the jury, that a young woman would plan the murder of her own sister more than six months in the future, for the gain of a mere £11 5s., a sum that would go but a short way towards setting up a home? (He did not mention that, for Mary, £11 5s. was almost a year's wages – she was paid only £13 a year by the Malonys.) Was it likely that the accused, if guilty, would buy poison with which to commit murder from people to whom she was well known? The whole case rested on the identification of the handwriting, and he felt sure that the jury would not be satisfied that the case was proven. At no stage, he reminded them, had the accused behaved in the manner of a guilty person.

Mr. Justice Mathew addressed the jury. He summed up the cases for the prosecution and the defence. His closing remarks made it clear that he believed that Mary Ansell was guilty. They would have no difficulty, he suggested, in recognising that the handwriting samples were all by the same hand. He drew their attention to Dr. Stevenson's evidence to the effect that there was no difficulty in differentiating phosphorous poisoning from yellow atrophy, and that this was an example of the former.

After an hour and five minutes deliberation the jury returned to the court to say that they were unable to reach a verdict. The judge asked if there was anything he could do to assist them, but they declined; the judge ordered them to retire once more.

Over the next two hours the jury requested several documents be sent in to them, irritating Mr. Justice Mathew to the point that he threatened to recall them to the court and have all the documents read out from beginning to end.

The jury decided they had all the documents they needed, and shortly afterwards returned to the court to deliver a verdict of "guilty."

The judge made his approval of the verdict quite clear. It was impossible, he said, that they could reach any other verdict. He had never come across so terrible a crime committed for so inadequate a motive. He sentenced Mary Ann Ansell to be hanged.

Outside the court a distraught Mrs. Ansell became hysterical once more on hearing the verdict. Mary was returned to St. Albans Gaol.

On Monday, 3 July, Mary's parents were allowed to visit her. The press reported that it was an extremely distressing interview, which left the young woman in a state of great anguish. Two days later, on the Thursday, a representative of the Under-Sheriff had the unenviable task of telling her that her execution was scheduled to take place on the morning of Wednesday, 19 July.

For the next two weeks, strenuous efforts were made on Mary's behalf to save her life. Several petitions were got up, emphasising her youth, and the lack of an adequate motive. One of them included the names of over a hundred Members of Parliament. Suggestions were made that she was not altogether sane, though she had shown no outward sign of mental instability during the trial other than an apparent lack of awareness of the extreme gravity of her situation. Dr. Forbes Winslow, a well-respected specialist, gave his emphatic view that Mary was insane, and that the court had not properly enquired into that aspect of the case. The Metropolitan Asylums Board approached the Home Secretary, urging commutation of the sentence. A national newspaper attempted to prove Mary's insanity by phrenology.

Over the next few days Doctors Nicholson and Brayn from the Home Office visited Mary in an effort to establish her mental state. They examined her several times, and based on their report Sir Matthew White Ridley, the Home Secretary, declined to recommend the Royal prerogative of mercy. There was not, he said, a single redeeming feature concerning the crime. Bearing in mind the length of time over which the plan was executed, he felt that any clemency would lead others to believe that no woman would be executed in the future, no matter what she had done.

That there was a history of insanity in the Ansell family does not seem to have been considered, or, if it was, it was rejected as irrelevant. Caroline of course was institutionalised; three of the girls' aunts had died insane; and their maternal grandmother had suffered from mental heath problems. The doctors who examined Mary while she waited to be executed were not unanimous in their verdict: one of them referred to her as "a mental degenerate [who] ought to be held irresponsible in the eyes of the law."

Charles Cusworth, the foreman of the jury, was horrified to hear that Mary Ansell was actually to be hanged. During the deliberations of the jury, he told the *Daily Mail*, it was their frequently stated belief that mercy would be exercised. He believed that if Mary hanged, other juries would be less likely to convict in similar cases.

Questions were asked in the House of Commons; the Home Secretary held firm to his decision.

At 3 p.m. on Tuesday, 18 July, Mary's parents and relatives were allowed a last visit. Mrs. Ansell broke down with grief. Mary said to Mr. Ansell, "Do you forgive me, father?" "Yes, certainly my girl," he replied. "If I did not forgive you, how could I expect to be forgiven myself?"

Billington was the executioner. He arrived in St. Albans Gaol at 4 p.m. on that same Tuesday afternoon. He had travelled directly from Winchester, where he had carried out another execution.

Mary slept well that night, and in the morning she received ministrations from the prison Chaplain before breakfast. At 8 a.m. her female warders brought her to the lodge at the entrance to the women's prison and handed her over to the male warders. The scaffold had been erected in the van shed just inside the prison wall. Mary's step was firm, and as she walked she repeated the prayers of the Chaplain: "O, Lord, forgive me. O, God, forgive this miserable sinner." "That will do," said Billington; "Now be brave." He pinioned her arms, and within a minute and a half from leaving the women's prison she was hanged, the drop being calculated at 7ft 1in. There was no sign of movement, and it was announced that she had died instantly. At 8:02 a.m. the black flag was hoisted on the prison flagpole, telling the crowd of about two thousand people outside that Mary Ansell was dead. She was the first person to be executed at St. Albans for almost twenty years, and the last woman to be executed there.

At 10:00 a.m. the inquest was held at the prison. Mary Ansell was buried within the prison walls, completing, in the words of the Hertford Mercury newspaper, "the final scene in the terrible tragedy."

Except of course it was not the end of the tragedy. Mary and Caroline's parents had to live the rest of their lives with two possibilities: either Mary had murdered her own sister, and been hanged as a result; or Caroline had been murdered by persons unknown, and Mary had been executed for a crime she did not commit. Whatever the truth of the matter, they had lost two daughters.

Chapter Nineteen

Rose Gurney, Rickmansworth, 1911

If Charles Coleman was not clinically insane, he was at least disturbed. But that was not enough to save him from a charge of murder at Hertford Assizes in November of 1911.

Coleman was about 38 years old, and he had a string of convictions going back to 1897, when he was charged with the attempted murder of his landlady. He cut her throat as she lay in bed, for no better reason than his dinner was not ready on time. The charge was reduced to unlawful wounding, but he still went to prison. Before that incident he had had a string of convictions, including indecent behaviour in church, larceny, wilful damage, game trespass and assault. After 1897 came appearances before the courts for theft of a watch, stealing fowls and robbing a till. While on remand for robbing the till he had attempted suicide. Further charges followed: drunk and disorderly, several more thefts, assault, and finally the mutilation of a dog, for which he received a further six months in prison. He was released on Saturday 15 July 1911.

That evening he met Rose Anna Gurney, of Mill End, Rickmansworth, outside the King's Head public house in Watford. She was a middle-aged widow that he had known for some years. The pair travelled together by train to Rickmansworth, where they went for a drink at the Swan Hotel. From there they walked along the Croxley Road past Salter's Brewery. They were last seen together at a few minutes before 10 p.m., as they crossed the stile leading to the footpath to Rickmansworth Park.

The following morning at about 8 a.m. Katherine Attley and her friend crossed the park on their way to church. Beneath a tree they saw what they took to be the body of a girl; on investigation they found a woman somewhat older, covered in blood. They told the lodge keeper, who called the police.

Superintendent George Pear hurried to the scene. He found the body of a woman, lying on her back. There were two pools of blood about two feet from the dead woman, and her blouse and skirt were saturated with blood. Ten feet away was her hat, and a canvas bag lay three feet from the body.

Pear searched the deceased for a means of identity. He noted that she had no money, though a farthing lay on the ground beneath her.

Superintendent Wood was given charge of the case. After speaking to several witnesses he established that the last person seen with Rose Gurney was Charles Coleman. He accordingly dispatched constables far and wide in an effort to track him down.

Right: Superintendent Wood, who investigated the murder of Rose Gurney in 1911.

By 9:45 a.m. the instructions had reached Police Constable Clark of Mill End. He ran his man to earth at the Cock public house in Sarratt. As Clark entered the bar at about 1 p.m. he saw Coleman drinking a bottle of beer. The officer asked the suspect to stand, and searched him; he found a pocketknife. He told Coleman that he was under arrest on suspicion of involvement in the murder of Rose Gurney.

"What shall you bloody well want of me next?" replied Coleman. "If I had known you were coming I would have put my head under a train." He admitted being with Rose the night before, but said he had left her near the park with two men. He did not know who they were; Rose had spent so long talking to them that he left her to it. "I hope they bloody well hang me, I am not afraid to die," he went on. "Why don't you shoot me out of the way?"

Clark obtained a trap and took Coleman to Rickmansworth Police Station, where Superintendent Wood charged him with wilful murder. He denied the charge, and repeated his story of the two men he claimed he had left Rose talking to. He added that he had spent the night sleeping rough beneath a hayrick in the park. "If I did it, I should say so," Coleman told Wood. "I don't care whether you hang me or not."

He appeared before the magistrates the following morning. He seemed indifferent to the proceedings, as Constable Clark and Superintendent Wood outlined the case to the magistrates. Coleman was remanded for a further twenty-four hours. On Tuesday he appeared before the full bench of magistrates, and was remanded for a week.

Above: the Cock Inn, Church Lane, Sarratt, where Constable Clark arrested Charles Coleman for the murder of Rose Gurney. (author)

The inquest on Wednesday afternoon heard from Dr. A. E. Clarke that Rose Gurney had received multiple stab wounds, nineteen in all; some were of a minor nature, but others so serious that the woman would have died within one or two minutes. Two of them had penetrated the lungs, and a third had severed a blood vessel to the heart. The injuries, said Dr. Clarke, could not have been self-inflicted. The jury had difficulty in reaching a decision, but finally delivered a verdict of wilful murder against Charles Coleman. The coroner, Mr. T. J. Broad committed the accused man for trial at the next assizes in November.

Coleman's trial lasted only a day. He appeared before Mr. Justice Lawrance. Appearing for the Crown were Theobald Mathew and Holford Knight; Mr. H. A. Taylor defended. Dr. W. H. Wilcox from the Home Office told the court that he had found human blood on Coleman's clothing. Extensive stains appeared on the cuffs of his shirt, and he found signs that an attempt had been made to wash them off. He had checked the knife recovered by Constable Clark, but found it free of blood. Oliver James, a warder at St. Albans Prison, testified that when Coleman had left the prison on the morning of 15 July there had been no blood on his clothing.

Mary Peake said that she had seen Coleman and Rose Gurney together at the Swan Hotel; Henry Ginger told the court that he had seen them walking towards Rickmansworth Park. Coleman had bid him goodnight.

Superintendent Wood described the charging of the prisoner, and in answer to a defence question outlined his criminal background to the court. Taylor's intention in revealing Coleman's past was probably to show that the prisoner was insane, and not responsible for his actions. If so, it backfired.

The defence called Dr. Charles Parker, who had examined Coleman after the 1897 assault. At that time he had come to the conclusion that the man was not responsible for his actions, and was likely to suffer "fits of passion." The judge intervened at this point in a manner that can only be described as hostile both to the witness and the defence.

> His Lordship: Was he in a passion when he stole a watch?
> Witness: No.
> His Lordship: Was he in a passion when he stole fowls and robbed a
>   till?
> Witness: No.

The prosecution swiftly followed up by asking if Dr. Parker had any records of his findings; he had not. Had the court in 1897 found the accused innocent by reason of insanity? It had not, but Dr. Parker believed that his evidence had resulted in a reduction in the sentence handed down.

Several of Coleman's relatives described how the accused man's son had been drowned some fifteen years before. The effect upon him, they said, had been dramatic. It was on that day that he committed the assault on his landlady. Five or six years later he had met with an accident at the asbestos works at Harefield, which further affected him. He tried to kill himself, the first of several attempts over the next few years. He complained of head pains.

The prosecution called Dr. Dyer, Medical Officer at Brixton Prison. He told the court that he had studied Coleman over the period of about two months, and considered him sane. He was morose and sometimes depressed, but Dr. Dyer did not consider that this indicated any mental problems.

Counsel for the defence then addressed the jury. Coleman's previous offences demonstrated insanity, he suggested. He had attempted suicide on several occasions. If the jury decided that Coleman had killed Rose Gurney, a crime for which he had no motive, then he (the counsel for the defence) asked them to say that he had not known what he was doing. His conviction immediately prior to Rose's killing had been for mutilating a dog – could any man who did such a thing be in his right mind?

The judge summed up. He reviewed the evidence, and then addressed the matter of Coleman's sanity. On this matter he let his feelings be known in no uncertain terms. As far as he was concerned, the prisoner was responsible for his actions. The bias against Coleman was glaring.

The jury took seven minutes to return a guilty verdict. The judge donned the black cap and addressed the prisoner:

> Charles Coleman, after a careful and patient hearing of your case, the jury have come to the only conclusion which it was possible to come to, that you are guilty of the crime of murder. That you took the life of this unfortunate woman there can be no doubt – for what reason no man can tell – but that you did it there can be no doubt whatever. And I think there is still less doubt that you knew perfectly well what you were doing. Your whole history shows a career of crime for years, and there is not the slightest suggestion by anybody – except in the year of 1897 when an attempt was made to get you off for that serious charge of attempted murder – that you were not responsible for your actions. All I have to do now is pass the sentence which the law imposes upon me, and that is that you be taken from this place to a lawful prison, and thence to a place of execution, from which you be then hanged by the neck until you are dead, and that your body be buried within the precincts of the prison in which you have been confined before your execution. And may the Lord have mercy on your soul!

Charles Coleman smiled, and said: "Thank you. I am very pleased to hear it. May I see my friends?"

If anything indicated that there was something wrong with Coleman's mind, surely that was it. He seemed not to care whether he lived or died; rather, he preferred the latter. The judge granted his request for visits.

On 5 December Coleman's case came up for appeal on two grounds. Firstly that he was insane, and secondly that the judge had misdirected the jury. The Court of Criminal Appeal threw it out. He would hang at St. Albans Prison.

On 21 December, at 8 a.m., after visiting the chapel and eating breakfast, Coleman had his arms pinioned in the condemned cell, and was walked by two warders to the gallows. He walked with a steady gait, and seemed unconcerned as to his fate. The usual county and prison officials were present.

John Ellis and his assistant, William Willis, were the executioners. This, the last execution at St. Albans Prison, went off without a hitch.

Above: Grimstone Road Prison, St. Albans. Charles Coleman was the last man hanged there, on 21 December 1911. (author)

Chapter Twenty

"I suppose they will hang me, and I deserve it." Mary Boddy and George Hitch, Buntingford, 1911

Charles Coleman may have suffered from no more than depression; the killer from Buntingford who appeared before the same Winter Assizes in 1911 was, without doubt, not responsible for her actions.

Mary Boddy was charged with the murder of George Hitch, aged five years. Mary was 65 years old and married, with nine grown up children. She was well known in the town, and seemed very fond of young people.

On Tuesday, 17 October 1911 young George Hitch was on his way back from his home in Norfolk Road to school after lunch. He walked hand in hand with his seven year old brother James. It was a few minutes before 2 p.m. as they walked down Church Road. Mary Boddy was walking along Paddock Road, towards the school. As she came level with the two boys, she seized George by the neck and cut his throat with an old table knife.

George Geeves, a tailor, was several yards behind Mrs. Boddy, walking in the same direction. He saw what had happened, and called out. He got to the struggling pair as quickly as he could – he was lame – and pulled the child from Mary's grasp. He took the knife from her as the boy staggered some twenty yards down the road into the arms of Frederick Lill, who had heard Geeves call out and come to help. It was clear from the flow of blood that the young lad needed immediate medical attention, so Lill carried him to Dr. Fell's surgery. It was too late. George Hicks was already dead by the time he got there.

Constable Joseph Hunt was in the High Street when he heard of the assault. He hurried to Church Road, where he met Geeves, who told him what had happened and gave him the knife.

No one had detained Mary Boddy at the scene, and she had gone home as though nothing had happened. It was there that Hunt, with Constable Murphy, found her a few minutes later. He arrested her for the murder of George Hitch, to which charge she replied, "I don't know the boy. I have never seen him." Hunt took her to the Police Station. He did not, he was later to say, think that she had been drinking.

Above: Paddock Road, Buntingford, from which Mary Boddy emerged to cut George Hitch's throat.

It soon became clear that Mary Boddy had no recollection of the assault. Dr. Henry Dixon was called just after 4 p.m. to make a brief examination of her, and found her quite lucid and intelligent. He, like Hunt, did not think she was under the influence of alcohol.

The only observation Mrs. Boddy made was, "Oh dear, is the child dead?" When told that he was, she said, "Oh, he is dead, good God!"

Dixon made a more thorough examination that evening. He found Mrs. Boddy able to answer questions on a number of matters, and her memory seemed clear, with the exception of the afternoon's events. Her only knowledge of George Hitch seemed to be what she had been told by the police. She said, "Oh dear, what will they do to me now? I suppose they will hang me, and I deserve it."

Mrs. Boddy had been in trouble before. She had in the past taken a razor to her husband, and only that year she had served two months in prison for throwing a small boy, Frederick Ward, over the bridge into the River Rib. Fortunately the lad suffered no major injuries. By sheer coincidence, young Ward was a cousin of George Hitch. She had on one occasion tried to kill herself.

At the inquest Mrs. Boddy seemed confused, and distressed about what she was told she had done. The Coroner, after establishing that she had no evidence to give, asked her if she wished to remain. She chose not to do so, and was assisted from the court.

Right: Doctor Henry Edward Dixon, who twice examined Mary Boddy on the day of the murder. He found her lucid on most subjects though she seemed to have no recollection of the killing.

Dr. Fell testified that young George had suffered a four-inch gash to the throat, slightly to the right hand of centre. His windpipe and the arteries on that side were severed.

The Coroner told the jury that theirs was a straightforward task. They were not to consider whether Mary Boddy was mad; only whether she had killed George Hitch. They returned a verdict of wilful murder against her. At the committal hearing before the magistrate's court, Mrs. Boddy denied all recollection of the crime.

George's death shocked the people of Buntingford. He was buried in Leyston churchyard on Saturday, October 21. Mrs. Hitch was so distraught that she was unable to attend. A subscription was organised to defray the funeral expenses, and even though subscriptions were limited to one shilling per person, there was more than enough collected. The surplus was given to Mr. and Mrs. Hitch.

The trial on Monday, 20 November, was quite short. As Mr. Henriques for the Director of Public Prosecutions outlined his case, Mrs. Hitch became hysterical, and had to be assisted from the court.

As the evidence given at the inquest and magistrates' court was repeated, Mary Boddy sat hunched in the dock, her head bowed and almost invisible.

The only new evidence was that of Dr. Sullivan, the Medical Officer at Holloway Prison. He told the court that he had examined the prisoner, and that it seemed there were mental problems in the family. Mrs. Boddy's elder sister suffered from "nervous attacks," and one of her own children was an "epileptic idiot," who had died in an asylum at the age of nine. Mrs. Boddy herself suffered a number of attacks whilst in custody, and had done so for six or seven years in the past. She did not entirely lose consciousness, but felt giddy. She could hear, but not see or speak. He described her condition as dreamy consciousness, caused by a form of epilepsy.

With regard to the day of the murder, Mrs. Boddy told Dr. Sullivan that she could remember how she spent the morning, and had some recollection of preparing a midday meal. After that, everything was a blank until she found herself at the police station. She had had other similar periods of loss of memory, sometimes lasting several hours.

The judge's address to the jury was short. There was no doubt that Mary Boddy had killed George Hitch. The case rested upon the evidence of Dr. Sullivan.

The verdict, quickly reached, was a foregone conclusion. Mary Boddy was guilty, but insane. She was committed to an asylum for criminal lunatics during his Majesty's pleasure. The jury expressed their sympathy for the parents of the dead child.

Chapter Twenty One

Death of a Stationmaster, St Albans 1918

Jonas Ellingham was Stationmaster at St. Albans, a post he had held for several years. He was known as a kindly, hard working man of 61 years of age, and was liked and respected by his colleagues and friends. Eliza, his wife, was three years younger than he was. The couple had six grown up children, one of whom was serving in the army.

Jonas and Eliza lived in the Great Northern Railway Stationmaster's house in London Road, the garden of which was his personal delight.

Eliza sadly seems to have become unbalanced as she grew older, suffering from delusions that Jonas was unfaithful to her. As far as can be ascertained, she had no cause to doubt his fidelity. Her husband seemed too wrapped up in his work and his garden to have time for a mistress. Certainly their children were sure that her suspicions were without foundation.

In recent years Eliza had made several threats against Jonas. She had told one of their sons, John Adolphus Ellingham, that she would "do him in" on several occasions. So frequently, in fact, that when she carried out her threat he was only "half surprised."

On Friday 16 August, Jonas went home for his lunch as usual. To his colleagues' surprise he did not return, as he normally did, to supervise the arrival and departure of the 2:45 train. They found that the station house was locked up.

John Ellingham (known as Jack) had last seen his father alive on the morning of Friday 16 August. That evening at 6 p.m. he called again, bringing with him, as was his custom, the local paper for Ellingham senior to read. There was no reply to his knocks, nor when he rattled the letterbox.

When the Ellinghams' daughter Mabel got home at 8 p.m., she found that she couldn't get in, and asked the station staff for assistance. John Archer, the chief booking clerk, obtained a ladder, and with his help the goods clerk got into one of the upstairs windows, and opened the front door.

There was a strong smell of coal gas in the scullery, and they found Mrs. Ellingham unconscious on the floor. While others cared for her, Archer went to the upstairs sitting room, where he found the body of Jonas Ellingham.

There was blood on his head and face, which was covered by a cushion. The booking clerk called the police.

Sergeant Housden escorted Mrs. Ellingham to the infirmary. On the way she said to him, "What's the good of taking me there? If I get better they will only hang me. I killed my husband, and have tried to kill myself by poison, but I cannot die."

The afternoon's events swiftly unravelled. Jonas had been to the barber for a haircut, and gone to the sitting room and lain down for a short nap. For some reason Eliza snapped: she struck her husband repeatedly over the head with a hammer, which she threw in the coalscuttle. She then wrote two notes, one addressed to John, the other to Mabel.

> Dear Jack,
> Perhaps this what has happened will bring you to your senses. I will forgive you, Jack, as I know you were misled. Good-bye. God above knows what I have suffered.
>
> Your broken hearted mother.

This letter she posted, and John received it the following morning. Mabel's letter she left on the kitchen table.

> Dear Mabel,
> I am sorry for you all. With your father's money and mine you may be able to do without going out to earn your living – not like poor me who had to work to help buy this house and in my old days I have no love or comfort, so good-bye to all. I am taking him with me.

An inquest was opened on Tuesday 20 August. Dr. Bates, who had examined the body, told the court that he had found seven puncture wounds in Jonas Ellingham's skull. He judged that a "blunt instrument" had been used. The Doctor noted that there was a blackened blood clot on the dead man's face, leading him to the conclusion that acid had been poured onto it. Detective Sergeant Paine testified that he had found a beer bottle containing what he referred to as "spirits of salt." A recently used teacup contained the same substance.

The coroner referred to the state of mind of the accused woman, but told the jury that there was insufficient evidence for them to come to a decision on that matter. They therefore returned a verdict of wilful murder.

Eliza Ellingham appeared before Mr. Justice Bray at Hertford Assizes on Thursday, 21 November. Sir Patrick Rose-Innes K.C. appeared for the prosecution, and Mr. Ronald Walker for the defence.

The trial was little more than a formality. Rose-Innes in addressing the judge said that he understood that there was some doubt as to the fitness of the accused to plead. Dr. Francis Forward, the Medical Officer at Holloway Prison, was the only witness called. He had had numerous opportunities to study Mrs. Ellingham since 19 August, but he was nonetheless reserved in his opinion. The judge was more confident, and led both the witness and the jury.

Rose-Innes: Is she in you opinion in a sufficiently sane condition to plead?

Dr. Francis: I think she is fit to say whether she is guilty or not.

Justice Bray: But we want more than that. We want to know whether she is sufficiently sane to be able to instruct counsel for her proper defence.

Dr. Francis: I don't think she could do that to the full extent.

Justice Bray: I think the mere fact of her being able to say guilty or not guilty is not sufficient. You think she is not in a fit state of mind to give proper instructions for her defence at this trial?

Dr. Francis: I think not.

Justice Bray (to the jury): You have to decide whether the prisoner is in a fit condition of mind to enable her to plead; that means whether or not she is in a fit condition to instruct counsel as what her defence may be, and as to all the circumstances that took place. I don't think there is any reason to doubt the doctor's evidence, because he has had ample opportunity of keeping her under supervision, and in that time ought to be quite able to judge. If you accept his evidence you will find that the prisoner is unfit to plead.

Unsurprisingly the jury quickly reached the desired verdict, and Mr. Justice Bray ordered that Eliza Ellingham be detained during his Majesty's pleasure.

It is possible that Bray had in mind the outcry that occurred when Mary Ansell was hanged. He was probably right if he thought that the protests would be repeated. The country had had enough death during the Great War of the preceding four years, and was in no mood for more. It was so much easier to lock the woman away, and forget about the whole affair.

Chapter Twenty Two

"I Picked up the Gun and Shot Him..." Ickleford 1939

The story of the shooting of 55 year old Harry Cooper begins some days before his death. Eric and Fred Wilshere had allegedly been trespassing on Cooper's land, and he had complained. The lads were two of three brothers, the other being Bob. Fred was married and lived away from home. Bob and Eric lived with their sister in Turnpike Lane, Ickleford.

On 15 August 1939, a Police Constable visited Turnpike Lane with a complaint against Eric and Fred for trespass. The following evening the three brothers argued, Fred and Bob came to blows over the matter. Fred was put out of the house.

On the 17th, Bob decided to stay in for the evening to avoid trouble, but the next day he met Fred and Eric at about 7.00 p.m. in a lane just inside the parish of Pirton.

The argument resumed, with Fred pointing out the injuries he had received two days before. It was not long before they came to blows again., and it was at this point that Cooper became involved. He had been cutting barley in one of his fields (he had leased Westmill Farm from the Council for the last 26 years). He knew the Wilsheres, and at the Coroner's inquest it was suggested that when he left the field and entered the lane, his intention was to break up the fight.

Exactly what happened next is a little blurred. It was suggested that Eric attempted to halt Cooper's intervention. True or not, somehow Cooper and Eric came to blows; Eric said that Cooper had struck him, and kicked him in the mouth as he lay on the ground. Other witnesses recalled seeing Cooper sitting astride Eric, and striking him with his fists. At some point Fred and Bob told Cooper that the matter was a family concern, and that he should keep out of it.

Fred was reported to have said, "Get the gun, Eric, and shoot the pair of them." It was never fully explained what he had meant by "the pair of them." Was it Bob Wilshere and Harry Cooper?

In any event, Cooper and Eric went into the barley field. Eric picked up a piece of iron - part of a reaper - but discarded it at once in favour of Cooper's double-barrelled twelve-bore shotgun.

Above: Harry Cooper, whose interference in a family dispute led to his death.
(Hitchin Pictorial)

Eric broke the gun to check whether it was loaded, then closed it again and pointed it at Cooper. One of the men working in the field, William Chamberlain, called out, "Put that gun down." Eric aimed the weapon at Chamberlain, who ducked down behind the binder with which he was working. Eric swung the gun back to Cooper.

It was then that, from a range of five or six yards, nineteen-year-old Eric Wilshere shot Harry Cooper in the chest.

When the police arrived, Inspector H. Smith approached Eric, who had apparently made no attempt to escape. Smith said, "I am a police inspector. I am given to understand you fired the shot that killed Harry Cooper."

Eric replied, "He hit me and kicked me, and I picked up the gun and shot him."

The inquest was held before nine jurors on the following Monday to hear medical evidence. The injuries were substantial, and described in graphic detail.

The fatal wound was between three and four inches wide in Cooper's chest. Some 94 shot wounds were counted during the autopsy. The breast bone was pulped, and though the membrane of the heart was perforated, that organ was almost undamaged. The large blood vessels at the base of the heart were shattered however, and the cause of death was the massive haemorrhage that resulted. The left lung was peppered with shot, and several pellets were found as high as the neck. The palm of Cooper's left hand had been blown away, indicating that he had raised his arm, perhaps as a reflex defensive action, just as the shot was fired. The shirt around the wound was soaked in blood, and there were bloodstains on the shirtsleeves and trousers. The dead man's face was bloodstained too, apparently from blood running from his mouth. There was no blackening around the wounds, confirming that the shot had not been fired from point-blank range.

As Eric Wilshere had already been charged with murder, and been remanded in custody by the magistrates, the coroner discharged the jury.

At the committal proceedings, Mr. Crump outlined the case for the Crown. There was no doubt that Eric had shot Cooper. He admitted it. His defence was that he had fired in self defence after having been assaulted by Cooper. This defence was damaged by the testimony of Roy Cannon.

Cannon said that he saw Cooper re-enter the field ahead of Eric - if this were true, Eric could not claim that Cooper was chasing him. Further, Cannon quoted Eric as saying after the shot had been fired, "It's a good job. I will hang for him. If there had been another cartridge I would have shot the other one."

There is an echo here of the comment attributed to Fred in the lane: "Get the gun, Eric, and shoot the pair of them."

The evidence of a local gunsmith, Charles Barham, showed that the gun was not faulty, and could not have fired accidentally. The constable that had taken possession of the gun stated that only the right-hand barrel had been loaded. Several other witnesses testified, but they added little to the evidence.

Bob Wilshere collapsed in the witness box as he described the events of that evening; and had to be assisted from the court by Inspector Smith.

The court had heard enough. Eric Wilshere was committed for trial at Bedford Assizes on 7 October.

On the day of the trial, Eric was smartly dressed in a white shirt, with a grey suit and tie. He pleaded "Not guilty" in a firm and steady voice. Mr. Maurice Healey, K. C., outlined the case for the Crown. He explained the background of the argument between the three Wilshere brothers, and ran through the events leading up to the shooting. Eric's statement made at the Police Station to the effect that he had fired in self defence was read out.

On the second day, Mr. Richard O'Sullivan for the defence offered no evidence. He submitted that the prosecution had failed to show that the shooting of Cooper was intentional and without provocation. Cooper was "an older and more powerful man, and he overpowered and beat - I don't say mercilessly - but he punched Wilshere." The shot was fired, said O'Sullivan, in self defence.

The jury disagreed, and found Eric Ronald Wilshere "guilty of wilful murder, with a strong recommendation to mercy on account of his youth, and because of undue influence." The appeal for mercy was ignored by Mr. Justice Singleton, and he sentenced Eric to death. Eric's defence immediately lodged an appeal.

The case came before the Court of Criminal Appeal early in November. O'Sullivan said that at the trial the defences had been manslaughter and self-defence. He no longer intended to argue the case for self defence, but that the verdict should have been manslaughter. He submitted that the trial judge had admitted evidence that was inadmissible, and that he had misdirected the jury.

On the first point, O'Sullivan submitted that the trial judge should not have admitted Fred's outburst, "Get the gun, Eric, and shoot the pair of them." He maintained that it must have been Fred's words that the jury was thinking of when they spoke of "undue influence." If the jury had believed that Eric had killed Cooper as a result of an instruction to do so by his brother, then a verdict of murder was correct. But as Fred's words were inadmissible as evidence, then the jury should not have considered them, and their verdict would have been different.

Had the jury accepted Eric's statement, made shortly after the shooting - "He hit me and kicked me so I picked up the gun and shot him" - then it would be reasonable to believe that the killing was done in the heat of the moment, and under provocation. If that were the case, then manslaughter would be a proper verdict.

The trial judge, in O'Sullivan's submission, had not adequately directed the jury on either of these two crucial matters. The Appeal judges disagreed. They did not even wait for the Crown to present its rebuttal of the appeal. There had been no misdirection, and the appeal was dismissed. The sentence of death stood. The appeal hearing had lasted just eighty minutes.

All was not lost. The Home Secretary had to confirm the sentence, and had the power to recommend to the King that he exercise his prerogative of mercy. This is just what he did, and Eric Wilshere's sentence of death was commuted to penal servitude for life.

What exactly occurred that evening - what Fred had meant by "shoot them both," and whether Eric was acting on that remark or in the heat of the moment - we cannot tell. It probably helps not at all to know that one of Harry Cooper's contemporaries referred to him as "an irascible man...one of these days his temper is going to bring trouble to the neighbourhood..." Prophetic words indeed.

Chapter Twenty Three

Poachers, Poaching and the Twin Foxes

Poaching has its roots in the distant past. The Royal Forests were the preserves of the nobility of England from the Norman invasion onwards, and the poaching of game from them attracted extreme penalties; indeed, there were special laws and courts that dealt with offences in such domains. Later, the landed gentry established game parks throughout the country, creating more opportunities for both the hungry and the greedy.

The word "poach" came into use in the seventeenth century, and was derived from the Old French "pocher," a pocket, presumably for the hiding of game illegally obtained.

Poaching is one of those offences that have never attracted severe condemnation from the mass of the population. Wild creatures have always been viewed by many as fair game, especially by those who relied upon them as a supplement to their diet. The viewpoint of landowners has, understandably, traditionally been somewhat different. The law supported the landowners. It was, after all, they that wielded power - at the ballot box, in Parliament and in the courts.

It was in the eighteenth and nineteenth centuries that the wars between the poachers and the landowners' representatives, the gamekeepers and night-watchmen, reached their peak, though the offence was viewed a serious one before then. Poaching could be a capital offence, especially where the value of the game exceeded a shilling; a prosecution for grand larceny was then an option open to the prosecutor. Things rarely came to that, though, and the vast majority of offenders appeared before the magistrates, receiving a term of imprisonment in the local house of correction or the county gaols in Hertford and St. Albans.

There was great concern in government over the predations of poachers, but it seems they only knew part of the story. In 1827 the Home Office asked for details of convictions over the previous seven years from the magistrates' clerks. The Reverend Philip Hunt of Bedfordshire replied that magistrates were in the habit of omitting such figures from their returns, and that "in many cases not a tenth part, perhaps not a twentieth part of the actual numbers

144

of convictions which have led to imprisonment... have been sent to the Clerks of the Peace to be recorded."

Right: a detail from "Coverside," an engraving by Edward Landseer.

The Game Act of 1831 gave lords of manors and other privileged persons rights in appointing gamekeepers with special powers to protect game, and in 1862 the Poaching Prevention Act allowed police officers to stop and search suspects. Anyone found in possession of dead game had to prove that he had come by it legitimately, or risk two months in prison. The law forbade the sale of unlicensed game, though there were always unscrupulous innkeepers, butchers and victuallers prepared to provide a market for the fruits of the poacher's craft.

Clashes between the poachers on one hand and the forces of the establishment were common, and, as we have seen at Aldbury and Bennington, they were sometimes fatal.

The encroachments by poachers were usually by night. A wide range of methods was used to catch game. Snares might be set, or dogs used; nets were used to catch not only fish, but rabbits and hares too; hooks were used to pull birds from the trees. Ferrets were sent down rabbit warrens. Firearms were commonly used, though some of them so old that they were a danger to the user as well as to the target. Muzzle loading guns that had been obsolete for many years were in regular use well into the 20th century. The wealthier poacher might have a folding gun, designed for concealment.

The poacher might be a father merely getting a little extra protein for his family, or he might make a living from the offence. He might work alone, or be part of a large, organised gang. We have already met James Chapman, an itinerant poacher, and Walter Smith, Frederick Eggleton and Charles Rayner, who worked as a group.

Above: a relatively late 20-bore single-barrelled folding gun by Cogswell and Harrison. It fits neatly beneath a coat, and is of better quality than most. Below: the jaws of a mantrap, designed seriously to injure the poacher and trespasser alike. (author)

The landowners responded with extreme measures. From the late eighteenth century, mantraps were manufactured under such names as 'the crusher' and 'the thigh cracker,' and were set to catch the unwary; spring guns with tripwires were mounted in woods, firing a charge of shot that brought to an end the career of many poachers. Even if the victim escaped alive, the danger of infection of the wounds inflicted and a lingering death was not inconsiderable. Such devices did not discriminate between the innocent and the guilty, and sometimes blameless individuals fell prey to them.

A large proportion of the population was illiterate, and could not read the notices posted as a warning. In fact, the skilled poacher was the person least at risk from spring guns and mantraps. He knew the woods and fields, and he knew too what to look out for. Cases of poachers moving these alarming contraptions to turn them against the gamekeeper were not unknown.

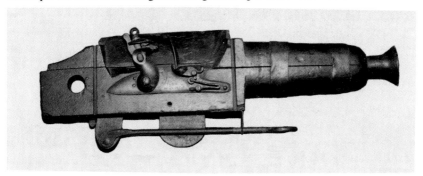

Above: a flintlock spring gun by Ive & Burbidge. The gun is fired by a trip wire with the intention of seriously wounding or killing poachers. (North Hertfordshire Museum Service)

Right: the more humane alternative to the mantrap and spring gun. When the wire is tripped, the barrel is free to slide down the shaft. The firing pin strikes the anvil, and discharges a blank cartridge. The device may either be suspended in a tree or forced into the ground. (author)

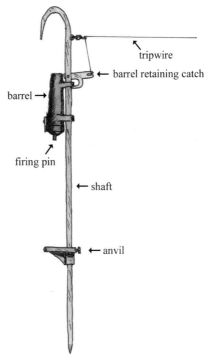

Devices designed to maim or kill were outlawed as the nineteenth century lawmakers responded to the mood of the times. As the punishments for other offences were reduced, so too were the sanctions that a landowner might employ to protect his game. In the place of the spring gun came the warning gun, which fired a blank twelve-bore cartridge when its wire was tripped.

Much of Hertfordshire was, and still is, rural, and poaching is a rural crime. It is unsurprising therefore that we find many prosecutions in the county.

There is in the Quarter Session Rolls for the year 1791 an interesting deposition. It was made by Joseph Ansell, who was a gardener from St. Albans. The document is an appeal for the justices at Quarter Sessions to intervene on his behalf.

According to Ansell, one Sunday he was walking with his terrier along a common footpath through Parlsey Wood, near Ruddick Hall, when he was stopped by the gamekeeper, Joseph Dynes, and his assistant John Cotton. While the gamekeeper searched him, claiming that he was a poacher, Cotton held a sword to his head. The two men tried to get Ansell to admit to poaching, but he refused to do so. They took him to Mr. Brand, a local magistrate, at Kimpton Hoo, where they held him in custody until 11 p.m. The delay was, he was told, because Mr. Brand was busy playing cards. When eventually Brand deigned to see them, Dynes said that there had been several snares set in the wood the previous day, and that he suspected Ansell of being the poacher. Brand asked whether any snares had been found on Ansell. No, there had not. Was Ansell beating for game? Again, no. Was the dog on the footpath? Yes, it was, but Dynes claimed that he had heard Ansell say "chew" to it. Brand decided that was enough to show that Ansell had been encouraging the dog to find game, and set the fine at £10.

But if Ansell was prepared to do Brand a favour... He wanted Ansell to catch a hare, and try to sell it in St. Albans. There was a lot of poaching going on, and presumably Brand wanted to find out who was prepared to buy game on the black market. Brand was not prepared to allow Ansell to catch the hare on his land however; steel traps and spring guns were set throughout his woods, he warned. Ansell was released, and told to come back in a fortnight.

When he did so, he told Brand that he had not caught a hare as instructed, and did not intend to do so. How did the magistrate expect a poor man to find £10 for a fine? As far as he was concerned, said Brand, Ansell could rob on the King's Highway for it. If he did not pay, he would go to gaol.

But Ansell had a trick up his sleeve: he had already arranged sureties to keep him out of gaol, and he would appeal to the Quarter Sessions against his conviction and fine.

Brand was furious. He claimed that Ansell had acknowledged that he had spoken to the dog, thereby confessing that he had encouraged it to hunt. He had therefore admitted poaching. The conviction said as much. Ansell could not therefore appeal. Unfortunately the outcome of Ansell's deposition is not recorded.

If Ansell's story is true, and it seems so bizarre that I am inclined to believe that it must be, it is an appalling example of the misuse of judicial power by a local magistrate for his own ends.

Before we meet the Fox twins, here are a few more examples of poaching in Hertfordshire:

1606	Thomas Pence	"…with certain dogs called spanyelles, and with a sparrowhawke," poached on the land of George Weale.
1666	Arthur West	To answer a charge of "shouting a gunn at unlawfull game."
1675	William Bassill	Six months imprisonment for "unlawfull coursing, killing, hunting, and taking away one redde deare…"
1681	William Hearde and William Martyn	Theft of a deer from Esquire Bernerd's park. The skin was sold to a glover at Hertford.
1701	James Nicholls	Convicted of stealing six trout from a river belonging to Philip Boteler. Nicholls was whipped in Hertford market place.
1716	William Thorogood	Indicted for taking "twenty fish called crayfish."
1732	Arnold Philbey	Taking trout and other fish from a pond the property of Thomas Aspinall.
1742	Jonathan Knightly	Netting carp and pike from the ponds of Lord Ashton.
1807	John Catheral	Hanged for poaching and resisting arrest. Considered even then to have been a savage sentence.
1811	Thomas Ghost	"…using a certain engine called a net to kill and destroy game."
1819	John Sibley	Poaching with a gun on the property of the Earl of Bridgewater.
1828	William Andrew	Seven years transportation for poaching.
1831	George Burgin	Three months gaol for destroying a pheasant by night.

1832	James Gower	Fourteen days in Berkhamsted bridewell for attempting to take and destroy fish from private water.
1872	William Squires	Seven years in gaol for night poaching and assaulting a gamekeeper.
1891	James Chappell and Patrick Williams	Indicted for trespassing in search of game, and assault of a gamekeeper.

The most famous of Hertfordshire poachers were the Fox twins, Albert Ebenezer and Ebenezer Albert.

The two brothers were born in 1857, the sons of Henry and Charlotte Fox, a deeply religious family that worshipped at the Ebenezer Strict Baptist Chapel in Albert Street, Stevenage, hence the names the boys received. They lived at Ten Acre Farm, Symonds Green, on the outskirts of the town to the west.

The two lads were identical, and their mother resorted to tying different coloured ribbons on them in order to tell them apart. Their similarity was to become a serious problem for the courts.

By the age eleven they were already setting snares and gin traps. At the age of thirteen they were caught in possession of a stolen gun on private land. The case was ably defended, and the charges dismissed. A month later they were caught again and fined 10s. It was the beginning of a life-long career.

Above: the famous, or infamous, Fox twins: Ebenezer Albert and Albert Ebenezer. Or perhaps the other way round.

For many years they attempted to thwart justice by poaching separately; if Albert was caught, he gave Ebenezer's name, and *vice versa*. When the guilty twin appeared before the bench, the charge was in his brother's name. He would ask for an acquittal on the technicality that the charge sheet was incorrect. It often worked. But science caught up with them in the end, and in 1904 the Foxes were amongst the first men in England to be convicted on the basis of fingerprint evidence. Thereafter they were unable to use their favourite ploy again.

There are numerous stories of the Fox twins' escapades – how Albert paid off a £1 fine from the sale of game taken from the magistrate's own estate, for example. Or how a local lady of the manor offered him a sovereign a week and a brace of pheasants to stay off her land. Being an honourable man, he did so – but Ebenezer didn't.

For a while, in 1915, the brothers went straight, and worked as hod-carriers during the building of Stevenage Police Station. The period of honesty did not last, and they were amongst the first occupants of the cells that they had helped build.

Right: the Fox twins help to build Stevenage Police Station in 1915.

Popular with all branches of law enforcement because of their courtesy and vivid imaginations in the excuses they used to avoid prosecution, it was a surprise when Ebenezer was given ten years for grievous bodily harm. He had lashed out in panic at a gamekeeper to avoid arrest, a foolish mistake that cost him dearly.

Ebenezer never recovered from his incarceration, and, after a period in the workhouse, in 1926 he died aged 69. Albert lived until the age of 80. The brothers are buried in St. Nicholas' churchyard, great characters both. Thus ended the twins' remarkable career, in which they amassed a truly astonishing catalogue of poaching convictions: Ebenezer notched up 82 and his brother 118. Well over fifty guns were confiscated from them, as well as hundreds of snares and large quantities of netting.

Finally, I make no apology for including the following poaching tale from the early 1940's. It happened to my father, the late Dick Walker, who was better known for his books and articles on angling. Though the events took place in Norfolk, he was a Hertfordshire man born and bred. I quote the story exactly as he recorded it shortly before his death:

> Some of my colleagues and I did succeed in supplementing our rations by shooting a variety of wildlife, including grey squirrels, rabbits, hares and pheasants. On one occasion my driver Vic Page and I stopped twice on our way through Norfolk to Bircham Newton. We were equipped with a .45 revolver for which Page had a proper firearms certificate, and a .22 Remington rifle with a telescopic sight - with which I shot two pheasants.
>
> After shooting the second one we had gone no further than a couple of hundred yards, when out of the ditch covered with camouflage vines sprang one PC George Mortar, who stopped us and said, 'You will be charged with killing game,' and so on. Having examined our two pheasants he said, (and I quote) 'Gor bugger boy, you don't miss much, do you?'
>
> He asked to search the van, but we pointed the Webley revolver at him and said No, you mustn't, it's filled with secret equipment - which was true! He had the good sense not to press the point, but he did report us and we were charged with killing game without a licence. In due course we appeared at the Magistrates' Court at the Petty Sessional Division of Smithton and Brothercross in the county Norfolk; we pleaded guilty.
>
> The constable gave evidence in the most formal 'out-of-the-notebook' way. The Chairman of the Magistrates asked 'Have you anything to say?' to which I replied 'No, Sir, except the evidence that the constable

gave was not quite exact.' The Chairman said 'In what respect was it incorrect?' and I replied 'well, he didn't say: "I have reason to believe that you have just shot a pheasant." What he did say was "Gor bugger boy, you don't miss much, do you?" ' There followed what the press usually describe as 'laughter in court,' which went on for a long time and involved the entire bench of Magistrates as well as members of the public and press. Then the Chairman said 'Constable Mortar, is what the Defendant says true?' The constable stood up and said 'Yes, Sir' and sat down again. The Chairman conferred with his colleagues and said 'You will be fined £1 each - that is our usual price for pheasant-poaching - and you will remain at the back of the court until the Court rises.'

When the Court rose this gentleman, who was a retired Colonel, strode up to us and said 'Now, you young devils, if you want to shoot my pheasants in future do me the courtesy of asking my permission first, and you may come and shoot two or three whenever you want.' We became friends with him, and never abused his hospitality; we never shot more than we were allowed, and it did supplement our meagre meat ration for the rest of the war.

It was an interesting episode, and I have laughed about it ever since. It is the only time I ever got caught poaching, and I should have been more careful! It is not as if I haven't done much poaching: I am not ashamed to admit that from school days, through university and right through the war, I did plenty. It transpired that we fell into a trap laid by the Norfolk police to catch some Canadians who had been shooting at anything that moved with everything that they had, including Sten guns and even Very pistols. It was them, and not us, that the police were trying to catch!

Thus the penalty for poaching changed in 150 years from death, through transportation and imprisonment, to a minor fine.

Chapter Twenty Four

The Wicked Lady: Katherine Ferrers and Other Highway Robbers

For some reason highway robbery carries with it a glamorous image; even when the predation of these armed robbers was at its zenith it was so. Why they were fêted by their less adventurous contemporaries is not clear. Perhaps it was because they seemed to be striking a blow against a repressive society, or perhaps the reason was pure escapism. Certainly the pamphlet writers and the press of the time glorified their exploits, much to the disgust of the authorities.

Above: the popular image of the highwayman. Dick Turpin, at full gallop, escapes the forces of law and order during his epic ride to York. The truth was somewhat different from this colourful and romantic image.

The Wicked Lady: Katherine Ferrers and other Highway Robbers

Sometimes people in their bitterness or enthusiasm let their mouths run away with them, and they got into trouble. In 1692 Benjamin Clarke, of Hunsden, apparently unsatisfied with his lot, said to Jeremiah Mathewes and Robert Pitt, "I will go to Whitney (Captain James Whitney, a notorious highwayman, of whom more later) and rob upon the highway." The first man he would rob, said Clarke, would be his master. He was indicted before the Quarter Sessions; his fate is unknown.

The practice of waylaying travellers and robbing them is an old one. Edward I recognised the problem in the Statute of Winchester of 1285:

> And Further, it is commanded that all highways leading from one market town to another shall be enlarged, whereas bushes, woods or dykes be so that... no man may lurk to do hurt within two hundred foot of the one side and two hundred foot of the other...

Oaks and "great trees" were exempted, though the ground had to be cleared beneath them.

It is in the 17th and 18th centuries that the traditional highwayman came into his own, though the crime was still being committed in the 19th century. The availability of the flintlock in the 17th century gave the ordinary man access to a pistol that was far cheaper than the wheel lock that preceded it. Instead of a complex clockwork mechanism that spun a wheel against a piece of pyrites, the flintlock struck a shaped piece of flint against a steel frizzen, which was incorporated into a cover for the priming charge.

The highwayman was mounted and armed. He waited for his victims along the main roads, commonly out of London, though other parts of Britain suffered their sorties as well. Particularly popular were parts of the road with a steep ascent, as horses were forced to slow down for them. Hertfordshire was prime country, lying across several major routes to the north and northwest. The prey might be the mail, a coach, or persons travelling on horseback. Items stolen included money, jewellery, and even the travellers' horses. Anything of value might be lost to the thieves.

So great was the risk of robbery that travellers adopted various means of defence. They travelled in groups; they hid their valuables and money; and they went armed with horse or pocket pistols. Coaches and carriages carried men armed with pistols or blunderbusses. Horse patrols sometimes made life difficult for the robbers, as did offers of rewards for any that would inform upon them.

Information could be the highwayman's friend too, and many unscrupulous innkeepers were not above letting the robbers know of likely customers passing the night at their establishments. As they resumed their journeys, the unsuspecting travellers would find the plunderers lying in wait.

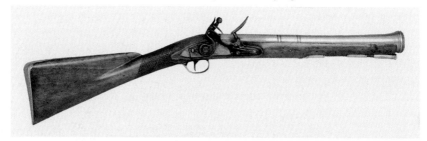

Above: An English 18th century blunderbuss. These weapons were frequently carried as a means of defence on coaches against highwaymen. They are best compared to large bore sawn off shotguns. (author)
Below: the blunderbuss was also used by the other side, as in this contemporary print of a murder that took place in 1682.

Though highway robbery was a capital offence until the 19th century, most highwaymen avoided killing those they robbed, even though "dead men tell no tales." It may be that they felt relatively secure; apart from the town watchmen, law enforcement relied upon parish constables, who were selected for a year's (usually unpaid) service. Those that could afford it often hired others to carry out their responsibilities, but the quality of some of these replacements was often abysmal. Some were illiterate, others infirm. Little wonder that the law was not much feared by criminals.

With so many genuine cases of highway robbery in its heyday, it is perhaps strange that the most famous of Hertfordshire's knights of the road may be nothing more than a myth. Nonetheless, the story has spawned two major films, with Margaret Lockwood and Faye Dunaway taking the starring role as "The Wicked Lady."

The story of Catherine Ferrers is confused, and there are several conflicting versions. Even her date of birth is uncertain, with variations of almost thirty years being given in different accounts.

She was born Catherine, or Katherine, Fanshawe, somewhere between 1634 and 1662. Bearing in mind the years of her reported activity, the latter date is the more likely.

When she was between twelve and fourteen, at her father's insistence she married Ralph Ferrers. Her new husband just sixteen.

According to legend, Catherine found life at Ferrers' family home, Markyate Cell, boring, and the marriage was not a success. In order to find excitement, she took to the road as a highwayman, riding a coal-black horse with white forefeet. Her first victim is said to have been her own sister -in-law, whom she relieved of her jewellery. Catherine's husband put up a reward for information leading to the capture of the robber, little knowing that it was his own wife who was responsible.

Tradition has it that she left the house on her nocturnal excursions via a secret staircase from her bedroom in the east wing of the house.

In 1683 she formed a partnership with another highwayman. His name was either Jerry Jackson or Ralph Chapman; perhaps he used both names. He was a local farmer in his day job, but at night he roamed the area of Watling Street (now the A5), robbing travellers of their money and valuables. Whether their relationship was more than professional is unknown. Shortly after teaming up with Jackson, Catherine shot a man who tried to resist their unwelcome attention.

According to one version, a servant at Markyate Cell saw her returning late one night, and agreed to keep quiet only if she gave up her life of crime. It was during this period that Jackson was captured whilst working alone, and hanged in 1684.

The servant died not long afterwards, and Ferrers went back on the road. She met her nemesis during a bungled robbery of a tumbril at Nomansland Common, near Wheathampstead. Unknown to her, there were two armed men apart from the driver aboard the carriage she was trying to rob. They fired, mortally wounding her. She managed to reach home, but died at the foot of the east wall of the house, where her body was found the following morning.

Her family buried her in the churchyard of St. Mary's Church at Ware, though not in the family vault: the damage she had done to the family name was too great for that.

The house still stands, though it was substantially rebuilt in the 19th century, and is now known as Cell Park. Parts of it are said to date from 1145, when Geoffrey of St. Albans founded a Benedictine priory there. In 1840, a Mr. Adey, the owner, discovered a stone staircase leading to an oak door, behind which was a small chamber inhabited by bats. Nothing else was found.

Unsurprisingly, Catherine's ghost is said still to haunt both Markyate Cell and Nomansland Common where she was shot; and there is a popular legend that her spoils were never recovered. There is a clue as to where they might be, however. A local riddle runs:

> *Near the Cell there is a well*
> *Near the well there is a tree*
> *And 'neath the tree the treasure be.*

Of the better-documented highway robbers of Hertfordshire, the most well known were the self-styled "Captain" James Whitney and Robert Snooks.

Whitney killed both men and horses (he stabbed them to hinder pursuit), and despite his glorification in a number of contemporary pamphlets he was a most unsavoury character.

Born in Stevenage in about 1660, Whitney's apprenticeship as a butcher in Hitchin led directly to his first criminal activity - cattle theft. It seems that he suggested to his master that they steal a calf that he, the master, had failed to obtain by lawful means. According to the story (and it may be no more than a myth), the owner of the calf got wind of their intent. He borrowed a performing bear, and put it in the stall that the calf usually occupied. That night the would-be thief felt his way into the barn and to the stall where he expected to find a docile calf. It was with considerable difficulty that his master extricated him from the claws of the irritated bear.

For a while Whitney ran the George Inn in Cheshunt. It was here that he became acquainted with highwaymen, and he sold up. He bought a horse and took to the road as part of a gang, working the highways from London to Doncaster. According to one account, his favourite area of operation was the road between Barnet and St. Albans. In November of 1692 Whitney and his gang got their largest ever haul – about £15,000 of tax money, taken in a robbery at South Mimms Wash. Dragoons were drafted in to hunt the gang.

Whitney was eventually betrayed by the madam of a bawdy house, and he was condemned to hang at Tyburn. He received a temporary reprieve when he offered to betray a non-existent Jacobite plot, but was finally executed on 19 December 1694.

Right: "The True Likeness of James Whitney, the Notorious Highwayman." This print is from one of many accounts glorifying the deeds of such men.

The True Effigies of James Whitney the Notorious Highwayman

Robert Snooks was one of the last of the old style of highwaymen. Born in Hungerford, he operated in the Hemel Hempstead area at the turn of the 19th century. In 1800 he robbed the mail close to Boxmoor, and escaped with money and valuables said to be worth more that £1,500; one banknote alone was for £550.

A price of £300 was put on his head, and he fled to London. There he tried unsuccessfully to pass one of the banknotes, and fled once more, this time to his native Hungerford.

In 1802 he was betrayed by an old school friend, whom he met by chance. On 11 March 1802 Snooks was hanged at the scene of his crime on Hertford's mobile gallows. John Page, postmaster and parish constable, was responsible for the arrangements.

Murder and Misdemeanour in Hertfordshire

As Snooks made his last trip to Boxmoor, he stopped for a drink at the Swan Inn. To some spectators travelling to the execution site he called out: "Do not hurry – there will be no fun before I get there."

At the gallows he addressed the crowd:

> Good People, I beg your particular attention to my fate. I hope this lesson will be of more service to you than the gratification of the curiosity which brought you here. I beg to caution you against evil doings, and most earnestly to entreat you to avoid two evils, namely "Disobedience to Parents" – to you youths I particularly give this caution – and, "The Breaking of the Sabbath." These misdeeds lead to even worse crimes: robbery, plunder, bad women, and every evil course. It may by some be thought a happy state to be in possession of fine clothes and plenty of money, but I assure you no-one can be happy with ill-gotten treasure. I have often been riding on my horse and passed a cottager's door, whom I have seen dressing his greens, and perhaps had hardly a morsel to eat with them. He has very likely envied me in my station, who, though at that time in possession of abundance, was miserable and unhappy. I envied him, and with most reason, for his happiness and contentment. I can assure you there is no happiness but in doing good. I justly suffer for my offences, and hope it will be a warning to others. I die in peace with God and all the world.

As the doomed man stood on the cart with the noose around his neck, he offered his gold watch to anyone who would guarantee him a decent funeral. There were no takers, and the highwayman's body was buried where he died, in a shallow grave, bound in a truss of straw. An earlier decision to hang the body in chains had been overruled.

Such was the courage he displayed at the gallows that sympathisers returned the following day and reinterred him in a coffin. Two blocks of Hertfordshire pudding stone marked the grave. In 1904 the Boxmoor Trustees erected a stone at the site of his execution and interment.

A short selection of highway robbers and robberies of Hertfordshire makes interesting reading:

- 1592   John Hardinge and John Rowlande, found guilty of highway robbery and hanged.
- 1647   William Symonds robbed by a highwayman of a packet of money near South Mimms.
- 1716   John Hill of Digswell, a blacksmith, was robbed on 24 March on the highway between Barnet and Hatfield, between noon

and 1.00 p.m., by three men on horseback. They stole £3 9s. 4¼d.

1730   William Cannon of Barley, robbed on 21 October in Standon, by a man who put a pistol to his head and threatened to kill him if he did not deliver his money. He handed over £4 17s.

1733   Thomas Lewis of London, a sugar refiner, robbed on 18 August at about 2.00 p.m. He was travelling on the Lincoln coach, and the offence was committed between Welwyn and Hatfield. He lost more than eight guineas to a highwayman in a dark coloured coat, riding a bay horse.

1770   William Ward, highwayman, shot dead in an attempted robbery at South Mimms Wash.

1790   James Page sentenced to transportation for life for the highway robbery of Fanny Doo. He took a purse worth 1s. and 4s. in cash.

1799   Alexander Hobbs, alias "Joe the Hatter," was hanged on 19 March for highway robbery. He claimed to the last that he was innocent. He got his nick-name from his white hat band.

1800   James "Shock" Oliver of St. Neots was hanged for attempting to rob in Clothall two men returning from Baldock Fair. A shot was fired, but no-one was hurt. Oliver left a wife and two children.

1805   Christopher Simpson was condemned to death for the robbery of Richard Oakley, a farmer, of £7 and a watch, near Breachwood Green. His sentence was commuted to transportation for life, but he broke out of gaol and escaped in November.

1812   Luke Lichfield was sentenced to transportation for life for the highway robbery of James Bennett. He stole a 13s. silver bank token, 6s. in money and a promissory note for £1.

By the second quarter of the 19th century highway robbery was forced into decline by the growth of the railway network. Coaches could not compete with the comfort, speed or price of the new form of transport, and wherever the railways went the stage routes folded like packs of cards. The formation of county police forces at about the same time ensured that the highway robber's trade became less and less viable, and eventually it withered away in the reign of Victoria as an anachronism.

No chapter on highwaymen would be complete without mention of Dick Turpin. It sometimes seems that "according to local legend" there are scarcely a dozen inns in England that he did not either run himself, use as a hideout, or at least sleep in. Amongst them are the Fox and Hounds at Barley and the Roebuck in Stevenage.

Whilst Turpin did occasionally operate in Hertfordshire, it is almost impossible to separate the truth from the myth. He did not, for example, ride 190 miles from London to York at record speed. Many of the deeds attributed to him were the exploits of other highwaymen.

Born in 1705, Turpin ended his career on 7 April 1739 on the gallows at York.

Right: the stone erected as a memorial to Robert Snooks, highwayman, at the site of his execution and interment. (author)

Chapter Twenty Five

Miscellany

This chapter contains cases that meet one of two criteria: either there is not enough information to merit a chapter of their own, or they are minor offences. Sometimes they are both. There is no particular plan or scheme in their selection other than the fact I found them interesting (sometimes shocking), and could not bring myself to omit them.

"A Pittiless Mother…" Margaret Vincent, 1616

Margaret Vincent was born in Rickmansworth, probably the daughter of Thomas and Alice Day. The records are incomplete, but it looks like the Day family had been in the town for many years. Her parents were well-to-do, and provided Margaret with a good education, unusual at that time.

She married James Vincent, and moved to Acton, west of London. For some years they were happy. They had sufficient wealth to live comfortably, and the couple had two children. All was well until Margaret became involved in Catholicism. In fact any religion would have served. She became obsessed to the point of mania, and did all she could to convert her husband.

Finally one day Margaret Vincent's obsession took over. Her husband was away; she sent the maid on an errand. She calmly took off one of her garters and strangled her two children, aged two and five. Their bodies she laid side by side on the bed. The reason she gave for killing the children was that she wanted to send their souls to heaven, where she believed they would become saints.

The deranged woman next attempted to strangle herself with the garter, but was unable to maintain sufficient tension to do so. She therefore tried to drown herself in a pond in the yard.

At this point the maid returned. She seized hold of her mistress, at the same time calling for help. Margaret's attempt to join her children failed.

The constable took her into custody, keeping her in his own house. A careful watch was kept over her lest she make any further attempt to do away with herself.

When she appeared before Justice Roberts, Margaret made no attempt to deny the killings. He therefore committed her for trial on a charge of wilful murder.

A modern prosecution would recognise that the poor woman was not responsible for her actions. The courts of the early seventeenth century did not see it that way. The devil and the "Romish papists" may have deceived her, but she was still guilty of murder. She was condemned and executed for her crime.

A contemporary pamphlet was published describing the events in detail. It condemns Catholicism as the cause of the disaster. An illustration shows Margaret strangling one child while the other lies dead upon the bed. A somewhat fanciful devil stands by, holding the garters used in the murders and encouraging her in her transgression. The pamphlet's title:

> A Pittiless Mother, that most Unnaturally at one time, Murthered two of her own Chillderen, at Acton, within six miles of London, upon holy Thursday last 1616, the Ninth of May, being a Gentlewoman named Margaret Vincent wife of Mr James Vincent of the same Towne. With her Examination, Confession and trew discovery of all the proceedings in the said bloody incident.

Right: Margaret Vincent, taken from the pamphlet, "A Pittiless Mother..."

A Case of Patricide, 1617

The previous case concerned a parent killing her children, but sometimes it happened the other way round.

Richard Terry and his son, also named Richard, were both tailors from Throcking. On 11 March the two men were playing shovelboard, and presumably Terry junior was loosing. In any event, he complained about the way his father was playing. His father ordered him to leave the house, but he refused, whereupon Terry senior struck his son, causing him to drop his money. Young Terry stooped to pick it up, and his father kicked him in the backside. Richard junior thereupon threw a jug at his father, fatally injuring him. He died on 27 March.

Richard Terry junior appeared before the Summer Assizes. The jury found him guilty, and he claimed benefit of clergy (see Glossary). Unfortunately for him he was illiterate, and was unable to read the "neck verse." He was therefore sentenced to hang.

The Killing of Margaret Bownes, 1617

The same year that Richard Terry killed his father saw a particularly cruel murder. On 8 September Margaret Bownes of Ware approached her husband William, who was working in East Field, with a petticoat she wished to pawn. William objected to her pawning the garment, and struck her over the head with a cudgel (value ½d.), killing the poor woman on the spot. He was indicted for feloniously killing her, found guilty, but claimed benefit of clergy, which was allowed. He thus escaped the full rigour of the law.

Whether William Bownes was a particularly violent individual or merely lost his temper on this particular day is not recorded.

Eavesdroppers, 1660

Ann Sickling of Ware, a widow, and Anne Packer, wife of Edward, were indicted for "standing as eavesdroppers, under the eaves of the dwelling-house of Joseph Scruby, of Ware, and for repeating what they heard there with the intention to sow strife and dissention between the said Joseph Scruby and his neighbour."

Marie Armstrong: a Lewde and Vagrant Beggar, 1675

A warrant addressed to the governor of the House of Correction at Hertford concerning Marie Armstrong is included in the Hertford Quarter Session Rolls. It speaks for itself.

> Whereas Marie Armstrong, an idle, lewde, vagrant beggar, was this 24 day of June, 1675, by Arthur Younge, of Kempton [Kimpton], Constable there, and George Williams, of the same Parish, husbandman, brought before me, Edward Wingate, Esq., one of the King's Majestie's justices of the peace in the county of Hertford, and charged as well with begging and idle wandering abroad, and also with other lewde and disorderly behaviours so as shee appears to be

dangerous to the people, and she will not be reformed of her roguish life.

These are, therefore, to will and require you to receive the sayde Marie Armstrong and her safely keepe in your said house until the next Quarter Sessions. And during that time she shall so continue with you that you hold to worke and labour, and to punish her by putting fetters and gyves (shackles) upon her, and by moderate whipping her as in good discrestion you shal find cause. Yeelding her for her maintenance so much as she shall deserve or earne by her worke and labour.

Above: Punishment circa 1685. On the left, whipping at the cart's tail, centre, the pillory, and top right, the gallows. From a contemporary print.

The Judgement of Sam Gregory, 1676

From a letter written on 9 July by Frances Leigh to John Chancy, a clerk of the peace, we learn of a case settled out of court (to Mr. Leigh's disgust). The interesting point is that the solution was reminiscent of the Anglo-Saxon system of atonement, or *bot*.

Leigh complains that he issued a warrant directing the constables of Barhamsted St. Peters to apprehend two men who "beat and dangerously injured" a third man. Sam Gregory, one of the constables, caught one of the two assailants, but instead of bringing him before a justice, he took him to the injured party. An agreement was reached between them whereby the assailant paid to the victim compensation on the understanding that he would not prosecute.

Even though Sam had "bin told that he did ill," said Leigh, he had not apologised. Leigh wanted him proceeded against at the Quarter Sessions, perhaps because he felt that his authority had been flouted. There seems to be no further record of the incident, so that may have been the end of the matter.

I cannot help feeling that justice was done: the victim was happy in receiving compensation, his assailant was punished by having to pay it, and the community was saved the expense of a trial. The only damage was to Mr. Leigh's pride.

Bribery and Corruption, 1682
Richard Barnard, Senior, of Hertford, who was a bailiff of the liberties of the Hundreds of Hertford and Braughin, was indicted for releasing a prisoner he had taken into custody for "a bribe of beer."

Dangerous Driving, 1690
Colonel Baron Tennynagall, a colonel of the Dutch regiment of horse, was quartered at the Bull Inn at Hoddesdon. The regiment was encamped nearby. Charles Fox was accused of assault and battery after he drove his coach and horse at the colonel, causing him serious injuries. His motive is not recorded, but he may have been a supporter of James II, whom Parliament had deemed to have abdicated the year before. James had been replaced on the throne by Mary and her Dutch husband, William.

Sarah Stout - Murder or Suicide? 1699
Much has been written about the death of Sarah Stout, so I have restricted myself to no more than a brief account of the events. The Stouts were a Quaker family living in Hertford. The head of the family, John, was a maltster, but he had died a few years earlier. He left a wife, Mary, and two children: Sarah and her younger brother.

Spencer Cowper was the younger brother of William Cowper, the Whig chancellor, and a budding politician in his own right. As a friend he assisted the Stouts after John's death, acting as a financial advisor. In 1699 he was thirty years old and married.

Sarah nonetheless formed a great affection for him, and showed it whenever he visited the house. When Cowper found that she was telling her friends she loved him, he went to some pains to avoid her, but gossip spread.

In the spring of 1699 Cowper visited the family to make a payment due to them, and Sarah managed to get him alone. Exactly what occurred is not known, but the maid heard the door slam, and found that both Sarah and Cowper had left the house. The following morning her body was found in the Priory river.

Murder and Misdemeanour in Hertfordshire

The Coroner returned a verdict of suicide, but this was a perfect opportunity for Cowper's political enemies. Together with the Stouts, who were unwilling to believe that Sarah had taken own life, they pressed for the arrest and prosecution of Cowper. He, and three others, were put on trial for murder.

Part of the prosecution case was that Sarah's body had been floating, and she must therefore have been dead when she went into the water. In addition, there were some marks on her neck that suggested she may have been subjected to a degree of violence.

The truth of the matter was that, as Cowper pointed out during the trial, there was no evidence that Sarah had been floating. Her body was caught up on some stakes in the water when she was found.

Other evidence was presented that three men had been overheard in an inn discussing Sarah, and one of them had said that he had been having an affair with her. It was suggested that Spencer Cowper was the man who had made this claim.

The jury were not convinced by the evidence, and the defendants were acquitted. The verdict was not acceptable to the Stouts. They were convinced that Cowper had killed Sarah. A writ for murder was mounted in the name of her younger brother, but it was destroyed and out of time for reissue, and the prosecution failed.

A war of pamphlets followed. For some reason Sara h is referred to in some of them as Mrs. Stout.

> "The Hertford Letter: containing Several Brief Observations on a late Prynted Tryal, concerning the Murder of Mrs. Sarah Stout..."

> "A Reply to the Hertford Letter, Wherein the Case of Mrs. Stouts Death is more particularly considered. And Mr. Cowper Vindicated from the Slanderous Accusation of being Accessary to the same..."

> "Some Observations on the Tryal of Spencer Cowper, J. Marson, E. Stevens, W. Rogers, that were tried at Hertford, about the murder of Sarah Stout. Together with other things relating thereunto..."

Did Sarah kill herself after being spurned, or did Cowper kill her to rid himself of a troublesome lover? It is not impossible that the evidence concerning the three men in the Hertford inn is true, and that Cowper had been having an affair with Sarah. That in itself does not prove him guilty of killing her. It is equally likely that Cowper, realising that a scandal would hinder his political career, broke off the affair. Sarah was highly strung, and it later emerged that she had threatened to drown herself in the past; perhaps that morning, after Cowper had rejected her once again, she chose to carry out the threat.

The Robbery of Farmer Glasscock, 1762

Following a spate of violent burglaries of the homes of the wealthier members of their fraternity, farmers in Hertfordshire and Bedfordshire were in fear of their lives. The latest victim was Thomas Glasscock, who was robbed of the considerable sum of £300 by five intruders.

The breakthrough in the investigation came with the arrest of Ganzelous Miller in Luton. He admitted being involved in the Glasscock robbery, and went on to say that he had arranged to meet his associates that evening to select their next victim. Thomas Jones, the "noted travelling rat-catcher," and William Bossford were soon taken into custody.

Meanwhile in Gloucestershire, William "Fudge" Harrow was arrested by thieftakers (see Glossary). He had been living near Wotton, but decided to flee when he feared that the authorities were on his trail. Sir John Fielding's men caught up with him in bed with a female companion, and though he was armed they were able to take him into custody without a struggle.

Harrow, Jones and Bossford were tried and hanged at Hertford early in 1763. Miller's fate is unknown, but he may have escaped justice by turning King's evidence.

Hertfordshire's farmers breathed a sigh of relief.

The Camp Burglary, 1799

The Camps lived in an out-of-the-way cottage between Stanstead and Hunsdon. They were an elderly couple, so when their home was broken into by two thieves, they were unable to put up much of a fight.

The burglars caught them in their bed. Mr. Camp was beaten with a heavy stick, and cut on the neck and the backs of the legs, while his wife's stays were cut through her to the skin. The intruders told them that if they did not hand over their valuables, their throats would be slit.

Whether there was no money in the house, or whether Camp was a stubborn old man, no cash was handed over. The robbers had to content themselves with a few items of lesser value. After telling Camp that as far as they were concerned he might sit and bleed to death, they left.

How they were caught is not known, but Mrs. Camp identified two men, Criswell and Burgess, as the culprits. Criswell was a large, burly man who came from Hoddesdon. Burgess came from Ware. Mrs. Camp's testimony was damning. After a short trial at Hertford, both men were found guilty and sentenced to hang on Friday, 13th January 1800.

John Carrington attended the execution, and recorded the event in his diary:

"The Gallows was carried from Hartford and fixed in the field near Camps House on the Right hand as you go to hunsdon, Supposed to be ten thousand persons their..."

As soon as the two men were turned off (hanged), Carrington and his companion went to dinner at Widford. Such was the callousness of the times.

Cruelty to a Child, 1807

Esther Gardener made a statement that during the previous winter she had visited the house of Ann Smith, of Cheshunt. There she saw the two-year-old Esther Warby, up to her waist in a pail of water. Ann Smith struck the child several times over the head, causing its nose to bleed; at the same time she swore at and threatened the infant.

Jane Vines said that some time later she saw Ann shaking and beating young Esther. She was shouting and swearing, and said that she would beat the child's nose to its face. The cries alarmed the neighbours, who noted that Esther's screams were much weaker than those of the other children in the house.

Eventually the abused child was taken from the house and given to Mary Griffin to look after. It was, she said, so undernourished and abused that she thought it might die. Its back from shoulder to knees bore the marks of repeated beatings. One ear was disfigured, and the child's nose was indeed "flattened to its face." One toe had rotted away from the foot.

There is no record of Ann Smith's punishment, if any.

The Robbery of William Henshaw, 1816

William Henshaw was from Dunstable, but one Saturday night he found himself in St. Albans, and it was raining. He was drunk, too, and a covered wagon standing outside the Red Lion looked inviting. He crawled under the canvas. Shortly thereafter he was joined by Charles Louch, a stranger to him; but such was the soporific effect of the alcohol that he dozed off.

When he awoke at about 4.00 a.m. both Louch and Henshaw's money were gone. There had been one ten-pound and two one-pound Bank of England notes, and about ten or twelve shillings in silver. Henshaw suspected Louch of the theft, and after a search he was apprehended.

Louch cannot have been very bright, because when he was arrested he still had Henshaw's purse on him, as well as one of the one-pound notes; he tried to throw it away when he was taken, but the attempt was spotted and foiled. The other notes he had passed to one Absolom Holt for changing.

Louch was indicted for the theft of the canvas purse (value 2d.), along with the money, at the Midsummer Quarter Sessions of the Borough of St. Albans. The Grand Jury found a true bill, and Louch pleaded guilty. He was sentenced to seven years' transportation.

He was held for some time at the Borough Gaol, at a cost of 6d. per day, before being sent to one of the prison hulks at Woolwich (an additional £3 5s. 6d. for getting him there). Destination - Australia.

Theft and Counterfeiting, 1819

George Child of Bishop's Hatfield, a labourer, was convicted of stealing a smock frock, valued at 3 shillings. He was imprisoned for a week, then publicly whipped.

At the same sessions, George Crouch of Wormley was convicted of passing three counterfeit shilling coins. He was given a six month spell in prison and two public whippings: once after three months, then again at the end of his sentence.

Assault in Baldock, 1846

On the 6 March 1846, Police Constable James Hawkes was called to an inn in Baldock known as "Stead's Tap," in order to deal with a disturbance of the peace. Whilst he was there William Carr, aged 27, came into the inn somewhat the worse for drink. It was he that had caused the earlier disturbance that had prompted Constable Hawkes being summoned.

Carr challenged many of those present in the inn to fight him. Hawkes, with admirable restraint, told Carr that if he did not leave quietly he would be arrested.

Unfortunately Carr was either too drunk or too foolish to take the hint, and Hawkes felt there was no option but to take him into custody. Carr struck Hawkes several times, then threw himself to the ground and kicked the constable's legs. The drunken man was eventually subdued and locked up at the station house.

The altercation resulted in Carr appearing before the Petty Sessions charged with assaulting a police constable. In evidence, Hawkes said that the only violence he had offered Carr in the exchange was to strike him several times on the hands as he had tried to pull the officer down by clinging to his legs.

Carr did not deny the offence, but said, "I did not know that I struck him – I was very drunk."

The jury returned a verdict of guilty with a plea for mercy. The Chairman of the Bench, Lord Salisbury, was not impressed by the plea. In passing sentence, he referred to previous convictions for assault in 1838, 1839 and

1843. Resisting a policeman in the execution of his duty was a serious matter, and he sentenced Carr to four months imprisonment with hard labour.

As a postscript it is worth noting that Lord Salisbury had been one of the most vocal opponents of the formation of a County Police Force only six years before. It would seem that, by his attitude towards assaults on policemen, he had by 1846 modified his opinion.

Rough Music, 1848

"Rough music" was a custom under which a community dealt extra-judicially with one of its members. The miscreant might be a scold, a person of loose morals, or some other minor offender. The local people punished the wrongdoer without involving the authorities.

In Walkern on 31 January 1848, a group of people descended on the house of a local woman whose morals were notorious. She was pregnant, and she had said that she would lay responsibility at someone's door though she had "been connected with many". It is important to remember that such a claim was a serious matter. The man thus named would be responsible for bringing up the child, and if it was another man's offspring, the selected man was unlikely to be delighted with the honour. A group of working men decided that the solution was rough music, ending with a ducking.

Unfortunately for them the authorities got wind of their intentions, and objected to the proceedings. The police arrived, and in the ensuing clash three officers were quite badly hurt. Warrants were issued for the arrest of those in the crowd who had been identified. There were counter claims that the police action had been heavy-handed.

At Hertford on 2 March all but one of the accused were convicted, and were sentenced to six months' imprisonment. There was a great deal of ill-feeling over the matter, even amongst the local justices. The view taken was that the woman was no better than she ought to be; that the police ought not to have interfered with a local custom as they had; and that the sentences were far too severe.

The police force had only been in existence a short time, and in a rural area like Walkern they were unlikely to be popular. Most country people believed that they were subsidising the force for the benefit of town dwellers. This skirmish cannot have helped to improve their opinion.

Grand and Petty Larceny, Late 18th Century

This small selection of cases of theft is representative of those appearing before the Quarter Sessions at Hertford in the last quarter of the 18th century. In every instance the trade or profession of the thief is given as "labourer," suggesting that the motive for the thefts was often necessity. Where goods are stolen rather than food, it is likely that they were sold on.

Year	Offender	Item(s) stolen and value	Sentence
1773	Joseph Steward of Great Hormead	worsted stockings, 10d.	private whipping
1773	Charles Sanders of Standon	bushel of wheat, 6s.	burned in hand, one month in gaol
1774	Richard Matthews of Much Hadham	hempen sack, 1s.	public whipping
1775	William Camphorn of Bishop's Stortford	bushel of oats, 10s.	transportation, seven years
1776	Thomas Gillion of Ware	bushel of horse beans, 3s.	public whipping, three months in gaol
1778	Charles Brown of Ware	unspecified quantity of wheat	work on Thames for thee years, or enlist as a soldier
1784	John Fisher of Braughing	Shoes and buckles, 10d.	private whipping
1788	George Ward of Widford	two pullets, 1s.	public whipping, one month in gaol
1798	Alexander Harris of Great Amwell	three pieces of rough oak, one piece wrought, 2s.	transportation, seven years

Other items stolen include linen shirts, muslin neck-cloths, china bowls and plates, small sums of money, a portmanteau (from the back of a coach), fowls, ducks, a pit saw, a set of copper scales, a harrow, an iron shovel, a linen bed quilt, an apron, a chaff knife, books, lead from a roof, a piece of bacon, and a silver spoon.

William Pigg, Farmer, 1903

Finally we have the case of the appropriately named farmer, Mr. William Pigg. It is particularly interesting insofar as his case shows the change in attitude to animals in the last hundred years or so. Bearing that change in mind, he seems to have been a highly-spirited character, with a sense of humour. Here is his story as it appeared in the press at the time:

A TEWIN FARMER SUMMONED FOR THREE OFFENCES:

William Pigg, farmer, of Tewin, was summoned at the St. Albans Sessions on Saturday on three different offences. The first was being drunk in charge of a horse.

Sergeant Pear stated that on Sunday, 19 July, at 9.00 p.m., he was on duty in the High Street, Harpenden, when he saw the defendant coming along on horseback. As he was swaying from side to side in a very dangerous manner, witness stopped him and found him in a drunken condition. Defendant commenced using very bad language, and so, with assistance, witness took him to the station, where, after staying the night, he was bailed out in the sum of £2.

Defendant: It was the best bed I ever had in my life (Laughter.)

The Clerk: Do you want to ask the witness any questions?

Defendant: No, go on with the case, I am prepared to pay. What we want is a new general manager of the police; we have got one for the railway, and it is about time we had one for the police. (Laughter.)

P. c. Hagger said defendant was using very bad language.

Defendant (excitedly): Ask my labourers if I use bad language. Be quick with the case, I want to pay my money, and hook it. (Laughter.)

The Chairman: Do you want to make any defence?

Defendant: I don't want to say anything. I only want to pay and get home. I am only wasting my time, perseverance and energy here. (Laughter.)

Defendant was then summoned for non-appearance to his bail at the last sessions.

Defendant: It was not my fault.

Serg. Pear proved admitting defendant to bail in the sum of £2. He was ordered to appear before the Bench last Saturday, but did not put in an appearance.

On being asked if he wished to say anything to the charge, defendant exclaimed "No, I only want to get on my horse and hook it." (Laughter.)

A third charge was brought against him for cruelty to a horse on the 9 July by riding it when it was in an unfit state.

Defendant would not answer the charge, but made some rambling statements to the effect that he did not ill-treat the horse; every horse on his farm knew him. He had got money in his pocket to pay, and was not afraid to stand before any judge or jury in the country.

The Chairman: If you are not quiet you will be taken out of Court.

Defendant: I don't care. I got a bed in the station before. (Laughter.)

Serg. Pear said that when they got the horse to the stable, they found, on removing the saddle, a large wound, on which the saddle pressed.

Defendant: The huntsman said he would never have a sore on his back in his life. (Laughter.)

Mr. Frazier, a veterinary surgeon, said the case was one of the worst he had ever seen. In addition to the wound on the back, the soles of the horse's feet were worn down so much that the horse could hardly walk. The lameness was in three feet, and on these the soles were nearly gone. It was caused either through the shoes being off a long time, or the horse had gone a long journey without shoes.

Defendant: When I started on my horse that morning it flew. (Laughter.) My son started with me and could not catch me, another started with him, but neither of them could catch me. It flew, but now it is starved to death, and all through the police.

A Constable (to defendant): Keep quiet.

Defendant: I shall not. That is Mr. Part on the Bench; all we farmers know him. I don't care for him. (Laughter.)

The Magistrates retired, and on their return the Chairman said that as it was the defendant's first appearance they would not send him to prison. He would forfeit £2 bail, in addition to 6s. costs; for being drunk he would be fined 10s. including costs, or one week's imprisonment, and for the last offence, the most serious of all, he would be fined £5 with costs £1 3s. 6d., or one month's imprisonment, a total of £8 19s. 6d. Defendant paid the money and left the Court.

Mr. Pigg the farmer seems to have been relatively prosperous as well as opinionated. His view of certain members of the bench would, I am sure, have been shared by other, less well-to-do, defendants appearing before it.

Glossary

Assize, Court of	a senior court, ranking between the Quarter Sessions and the King's Bench; or an enactment with legal force, for example the *Assize* of Bread and Ale.
benefit of clergy	a system exempting clerics and clergy from trial and punishment. The test was the ability to read the first verse of Psalm 51, which became know as the "neck verse." Later used as a means of showing mercy for a first offence.
bridewell	see *house of correction.*
Commission of the Peace	appointment of justices to hold sessions for the keeping of the peace within a county or liberty.
common law	law based originally upon custom rather than statute.
Coroner	the official presiding over an inquest.
County Court	either the old Shire Court under another name, or a much more recent civil court.
Crown Court	replacement for the Courts of Assize and Quarter Sessions in 1972.
drop	the distance that a condemned person falls when being hanged. The calculation is based on weight and height, the intention being to break the neck, but not pull the head off. Errors were made in both directions.
felony	a serious offence, originally meriting the death sentence.
Gaol Delivery	trial of prisoners held on criminal charges.
Grand Jury	a jury that decided whether there was a case to answer, and laid charges on behalf of the populace.
house of correction	a local prison, originally for confinement of rogues and vagabonds. Colloquially known as a bridewell.
ignoramus	a grand jury verdict meaning no case to answer.
indictment	a formal accusation of a crime.
inquest	an enquiry into a sudden, violent or unexplained death.
King's Bench	initially heard cases of royal concern, or offenders with a right to be tried by the King. In time it began to concentrate on criminal cases, though civil suits were still heard. It also corrected errors of lower courts.
King's Peace	either the peace of the land as a whole, or disturbance of the King, for which a heavy fine was levied.
liberty	a manor or a lordship with a charter making it independent of the hundreds.

misdemeanour	an offence less serious than a felony.
Petty Sessions	a court presided over by one or more Justices of the Peace.
presentment	a report by a constable or jury concerning a crime.
Quarter Sessions	a court between the Petty Sessions and Court of Assize.
recognizance	a bond for appearance or good behaviour.
rolls	records of a court, e.g. Quarter Session Rolls.
summary offence	a minor offence, normally dealt with by magistrates.
thieftaker	a professional thief catcher, who derived his income from rewards.
transportation	the practice of sending convicted persons overseas.
true bill	a grand jury verdict that there is a case to answer.
tumbrill	a type of covered cart or waggon
vestry	a form of local government, based on the local church administration, following the decline of manor courts.

Money and Measures

For those unfamiliar with the Imperial system of weights and measures, and "pounds, shillings and pence," here are explanations and conversions for some of those most commonly encountered.

Money

1 pound = 20 shillings
1 shilling = 12 pence
1 penny = 4 farthings
1 crown = 5 shillings
1 guinea = 21 shillings
1 mark = 13 shillings and 4 pence

Shillings and pence were often shown thus: 2/6- (2 shillings and 6 pence).

Land Measures and Lengths

1 hide = 4 virgates
1 virgate = 30 acres
1 acre = 4840 square yards
1 mile = 1760 yards
1 furlong = 220 yards
1 chain = 22 yards
1 yard = 3 feet
1 foot = 12 inches

Volume

1 gallon = 8 pints
1 quart = 2 pints

Weight

1 ton = 20 hundredweight (cwt.)
1 hundredweight = 8 stone (st.)
1 stone = 14 pounds (lb.)
1 pound = 16 ounces (oz.)

Conversions

1 metre = 39 inches
1 mile = 1.61 kilometres
1 acre = 4047 square metres
1 pound = 0.454 kilograms
1 gallon = 4.55 litres

Bibliography

Beachcroft, T. O. & Emms, W. B. *Five Hide Village* Datchworth Parish Council 1984

Billett, Michael *Highwaymen and Outlaws* Arms & Armour Press 1997

Bland, James *The Common Hangman* Ian Henry Publications 1984

Branch Johnson, W., Ed. *Memorandums For...The Carrington Diaries* Phillimore & Co. Ltd. 1973

Cockburn, J.S. *Calendar of Hertfordshire Assize Records, Vols I & II, Eliz. I & James I* HMSO 1975

Craufurd, Ruth *The Aldbury Double Murder* 1963

Curtis, Gerald *A Chronicle of Small Beer* Phillimore 1970

Dean, David *St. Albans Quarter Sessions Rolls 1784-1820* Hertfordshire Record Publications 1991

Denning, Lord *Landmarks in the Law* Butterworth & Co. 1984

Egan, Pierce *Account of the Trial John Thurtell and Joseph Hunt* Knight and Lacey 1824

Elmsey, Clive *Crime and Society in England 1759-1900* Longman Group UK Ltd. 1996

Foster, Anthony M. *Market Town* E & E Plumridge Ltd. 1987

Garland, David *Punishment and Welfare - A History of Penal Strategies* Gower Publishing Co Ltd., 1985

Gelish, W. B. *Hertfordshire Folklore* S. R. Publishers Ltd., 1970

Griffin, Ken *Transported Beyond the Seas* Hertfordshire Family & Population Society 1997

Haining, Peter *The English Highwayman* Robert Hale 1991

Harrison, Paul *Hertfordshire and Bedfordshire Murders* Countryside Books 1993

Hertfordshire Advertiser

Hertfordshire Express

Hertfordshire Federation of Women's Institutes *The Hertfordshire Village Book* Countryside Books 1986

Hertford Mercury

Hine, Reginald *Hitchin Worthies* George Allen & Unwins Ltd 1932

Hitchin Pictorial

Hole, Christina *Witchcraft in England* Charles Scibner's Sons 1947

Jones, Arthur, Ed. *Hertfordshire 1731-1800 as Recorded in the Gentleman's Magazine* Hertfordshire Publications 1993

Kramer, Heinrich, and Sprenger, James *Malleus Maleficarum* Braken Books 1996

Le Hardy, W. *Hertfordshire County Session Rolls, 2 Vols,* Hertfordshire County Council

Osborn, Neil *The Story of Hertfordshire Police* Hertfordshire Countryside 1970

Priestly, Philip *Victorian Prison Lives* Pimlico 1999

Pringle, Nik, and Treversh, Jim *150 Years Policing in Watford District & Hertfordshire County* Radley Shaw Publishing 1991

Thompson, David *England in the Nineteenth Century* Penguin Books 1950

CRIME IN HERTFORDSHIRE

Volume One: Law and Disorder

by Simon Walker

This volume covers the history of law and order in Hertfordshire from the Anglo Saxon period to the middle of the twentieth century. Criminal law, the courts, the punishments and the means of enforcement have changed over the course of more than a thousand years, and the author traces those changes, illustrated with examples drawn from throughout Hertfordshire.

He has included the unusual and the commonplace; from murder to highway robbery and petty theft. What is the truth about trial by ordeal? What happened to John Doggett who swore, "By God, he shot your dogs" in the 1600's? Take a tour round the prisons and places of confinement in the country; what were conditions like in the dungeon at Bishop's Stortford castle? Meet the "resurrection men," or body snatchers, the murderers, thieves, poachers and vagabonds. How was law and order enforced in the past, and how did the police forces of today originate? This book will appeal to students of both the history of crime and punishment and those interested in the history of Hertfordshire as a whole.

A Book Castle Publication

JOURNEYS INTO HERTFORDSHIRE

by Anthony Mackay

This collection of nearly 200 ink drawings depicts the buildings and landscape of the still predominantly rural county of Hertfordshire. After four years of searching, the author presents his personal choice of memorable images, capturing the delights of a hitherto relatively unfeted part of England.

The area is rich in subtle contrasts – from the steep, wooded slopes of the Chilterns to the wide-open spaces of the north-east and the urban fringes of London in the south. Ancient market towns, an impressive cathedral city and countless small villages are surrounded by an intimate landscape of rolling farmland.

The drawings range widely over all manner of dwellings from stately home to simple cottage and over ecclesiastical buildings from cathedral to parish church. They portray bridges, mills and farmsteads, chalk downs and watery river valleys, busy street scenes and secluded village byways.

The accompanying notes are deliberately concise but serve to entice readers to make their own journeys around this charming county.

A Book Castle Publication

HAUNTED HERTFORDSHIRE

by Nicholas Connell and Ruth Stratton

The most extensive collection of the county's ghosts ever written, with over 300 stories. Many are little-known and previously unpublished, having been hidden away in the vaults of Hertfordshire Archives and Local Studies. Others are up to the moment accounts of modern hauntings in the words of those who have experienced them. All supported by dozens of rare and evocative pictures, an outline of the latest theories and diary dates of regular apparition appearances.

Stories feature a feast of phantoms, including grey ladies, dashing cavaliers, spectral transport, headless horsemen and a gallery of Kings and Queens. Locations include Bishops Stortford, Datchworth, Harpenden, Hertford, Hitchin, Hoddesden, St. Albans, Ware and Watford.

A Book Castle Publication

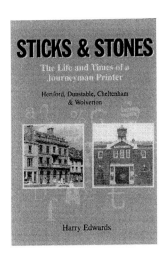

STICKS & STONES
The Life and Times of a Journeyman Printer
Hertford, Dunstable, Cheltenham & Wolverton

by Harry Edwards

Sticks and Stones recounts the story of the author's journey through his life in the printing industry, from printer's devil until retirement. Leaving school at the age of fourteen, Harry's transition from schoolboy to apprentice was abrupt. The printing world, with its own language, customs and traditions, was strange at first but most of the journeymen were kind and helpful to a young lad, covering up for many a mistake in the first formative years. The journey begins in Hertfordshire, then takes him on to Bedfordshire, Gloucester, London and finally to Buckinghamshire.

A Book Castle Publication

BUCKINGHAMSHIRE MURDERS

by Len Woodley

Thoroughly researched accounts of seventeen murders ranging across the old County of Buckinghamshire. Commencing from the early nineteenth century right up to modern times. You will read about the Newton Longville shop-keeper murdered for a few shillings; the Dagnall killer; murders for no apparent reason at Buckingham and Denham; the unsolved murder of the canal man at Slough; love affairs that went tragically wrong at Burnham and Bourne End; a fatal ambush at Botolph Claydon; the Pole who wanted to be shot and a fellow country-man who escaped justice by fleeing to the Soviet Union. There is the trooper who slew his girlfriend at Slough and hid the body under the mattress; the W.R.A.F. girl who offered to baby-sit but met a killer instead; the bright young girl who went for a last walk down a country lane and the couple who were the victims of a man's obsession with himself!

A Book Castle Publication

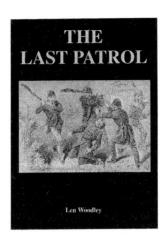

THE LAST PATROL
Policemen Killed on Duty while Serving in the Thames Valley
by Len Woodley

This book details those Policemen who have been killed on duty by a criminal act within the area now covered by the Thames Valley Police - namely the counties of Berkshire, Buckinghamshire and Oxfordshire. It ranges from a Constable who, in the 1860s, died in Oxford just days after the formation of one of the constituent forces that made up the present-day Thames Valley Police and must surely be one of the shortest serving Policemen in this country, to the truly terrible day at Hungerford in the late 1980s, when so many people, including a traffic Constable, were murdered and others wounded in that picturesque Berkshire town. It encompasses Police officers encountering poachers, ejecting some drunken men from a public house, checking details of members of the visiting forces involved in a fracas in wartime England, attempting the apprehension of burglars and questioning some vicious, "stop at nothing" criminals over their behaviour in a motor car.

These police officers all started their day as normal, not one gave a thought to the possibility that he might be sent to a life-threatening job.

A Book Castle Publication

EXPLORING HISTORY ALL AROUND

by Vivienne Evans

A handbook of local history, arranged as a series of routes to cover Bedfordshire and adjoining parts of Hertfordshire and Buckinghamshire. It is organised as two books in one. There are seven thematic sections full of fascinating historical detail and anecdotes for armchair reading. Also it is a perfect source of family days out as the book is organised as circular motoring/cycling explorations, highlighting attractions and landmarks.

Also included is a background history to all the major towns in the area, plus dozens of villages, which will enhance your appreciation and understanding of the history that is all around you!

A Book Castle Publication

SUGAR MICE AND STICKLEBACKS

by Harry Edwards

Memories of a typical English village, Hertingfordbury, in the pre-war days when life was slower and gentler... When the grocer, baker, cobbler, tailor, post-office, sweet-shop and builder's yard were all close at hand; the milk was delivered in a horse drawn cart. Facilities included a village school, a branch-line railway station, a Memorial Hall, a cricket pitch and pavilion, and the imposing Church of St. Mary with its Old Rectory. A vivid picture of country life is conjured up.

Harry Edwards was born in a cottage next to the mill, and enjoyed a close family life. The luxuries of his mother's home-made cakes and pastries, his father's home grown produce, the early impact of radio and eventually main sewerage! The occasional spectacular flying displays nearby were a welcome diversion, as were visits to the village by Cycling Touring Club groups of fifty or so people, resplendent in their plus-fours.

Boyhood pleasures only needed a simple stick or ball; hours of fun could be found just in sorting out mother's button tin; or a more ambitious project could lead to a rickety trolley or punt. A special joy to Harry as a youngster was splashing about with the gang in the endlessly fascinating river - or fishing by jar for sticklebacks in the extensive watercress beds.

A Book Castle Publication

MYSTERIOUS RUINS
The Story of Sopwell Priory St Albans
by Donald Pelletier

Ask people about the Ruins of Sopwell and they may say, "That's the spooky place" or "That's where I love to go and spend some quiet time". Few realise that the site has so many intriguing tales to tell.

Once a cell of St. Albans Abbey, The Benedictine Priory's most famous nun, Dame Juliana Berners, is still an icon to fly-fishermen worldwide today - why? Did Henry VIII and Anne Boleyn marry in secret at Sopwell? After the Dissolution and Robert Lee's rebuilding, how do the Sadleir and Pemberton families, the founder of Rhode island, the duke of Marlborough and Sir Francis Bacon fit into the story? Where are the re-discovered Holy Well, the re-located ceiling medallions and the missing church arch?

Across the fields from St. Albans Cathedral, Sopwell is indeed a sight of many mysteries. Why not visit the ruins and experience the unique atmosphere for yourself?

A Book Castle Publication